MW00961399

AND
CONFESS

How I Came to Declare
"in statu confessionis"
Against an Idolatrous Institution —
the Evangelical Lutheran Church in America (ELCA)

By the Reverend Timothy J. Swenson

with other subscribers

"In Statu Confessionis"

To declare that one is *in statu confessionis* is to pronounce a state of confessional protest against a "churchly" entity which has become heterodox, such an entity being in violation of Scripture and the Lutheran Confessions. This declared critical state of affairs is a public, churchly, and confessional form of protest and is the most potent type of protest that can be made. To declare a *status confessionis* is a solemn and weighty matter. It is an exercise of the office of the keys.

To declare a state of confessional protest is something done
- for the sake of the saving Gospel of Christ
- pastorally in concern for the faith of those in error
- for preserving the pure preaching of the Gospel and the right administration of the holy sacraments in the Church.
- to bring to repentance those who have fallen into false doctrine and errant practice.

This state of confessional protest is exhibited by
- severing fellowship with those in one's church body which teach false doctrine and those which support false teaching
- suspending pulpit fellowship provisionally with those pastors and church officials of one's own church body which propagate false doctrine either actively or through passivity (2 Thess. 3:13-15; Romans 16:17).

To declare a *status confessionis* means
- to cease and desist from all activities of word and deed which support the ministry of those within one's church body who are propagating false doctrine actively or by indifference.
- that being *in statu confessionis* is only to be a temporary condition in which the orthodox party remains under affliction until either full doctrinal orthodox is reached or is summarily rejected in unrepentance.[1]

STAND AND CONFESS

How I Came to Declare
"in statu confessionis"
Against an Idolatrous Institution —
the Evangelical Lutheran Church in America (ELCA)

Published by
St. Martin's School for Theological Discernment
Arnegard/Alexander, North Dakota
An academic and ecclesial affiliate of
Augsburg Lutheran Theological Seminary
Augsburg Lutheran Churches
http://www.augsburgchurches.org/

©copyright: Timothy J. Swenson
The Season of Advent,
Anno Domino 2009

ISBN 978-0-557-28806-9

TABLE OF CONTENTS

PREFACE *(start here)*
(Check out Word Alone's statement. On page 88)

My Confession

I confess to you, my brother and sisters in Christ, and before God my enabling of this current state of affairs and my inability to divert my church from its slide into heterodoxy, schism and apostasy. The ELCA's become an idolatrous institution: I Have Been "Unchurched!"

First, I confess my enabling:

- During the years of the Commission for a New Lutheran Church (CNLC) leading up to the formation of the Evangelical Lutheran Church in America (ELCA) in 1989, I was a supporter of the CNLC's work.
- Entering seminary in 1986, I found the campus rife with conversation about the potential of this "new" Lutheran body. Being back on the farm in the summer prior to the ELCA's incorporation and the subsequent decision each congregation had to make (or not make) to join, I heard numerous voices of dissent and attended meetings sponsored by both those dissenters and by church officials.
- Asked by many if I was concerned about the various "agendas" being revealed in the CNCLC's proposals, I responded that church history has demonstrated that—like a pendulum—the church swings back and forth. The church can be likened to river meandering between its left and right banks.

I repent my lack of concern and it's enabling of the events that have resulted in my church's subsequent heterodoxy, schism, and apostasy.

Second, I confess my inability:

- To be a more effective opponent of the agendas which have "unchurched" me;[2]
- To be a more generous supporter of the groups who opposed the agendas which have unchurched me;
- To be a more inspirational recruiter to the cause of opposing the agendas which have unchurched me.
- To more vigorously oppose those agendas and their supporters legislatively and structurally within the institutional life of the ELCA.

I repent of my inability to effect change within my church, the ELCA.

Therefore I ask forgiveness from those who have been "unchurched" like me and from those who have done the "unchurching."

Lord, have mercy!

Confession and Division

The time for talking has passed. The time for confessing is at hand. Division has been thrust upon us. No more time can be wasted trying to convince "hard cases."[3] Upon such hardened hearts only the Word of God can be effective. So I will declare the sweetness of the Gospel *("For I am not ashamed of the gospel, for it is God's power for salvation to everyone who believes"* Romans 1:16) into the depths of their error, announcing to them that our Lord Jesus Christ has forgiven them their sin. With that preaching of the Gospel, the Holy Spirit will "call, gather, enlighten, sanctify and keep them in the one true faith"[4] — which is Jesus Christ, **OR** God will continue to harden their hearts so that they may be bound to the consequences of their sin and thereby know the wrath of God *("Therefore God gave them over in the desires of their hearts to impurity, to dishonor their bodies among themselves. They exchanged the truth of God for a lie and worshiped and served the creation rather than the Creator, who is blessed forever! Amen."* Romans 1:24-26)

Confession: Action, not acquiescence

"STAND AND CONFESS!" invites my fellow members of the ELCA to join me in taking action. Those of us who cannot "ACQUIESCE" as this division is worked upon us will not be silently unchurched by an unaccountable bureaucracy.

- No more will we "DUCK AND COVER" hoping that the agendas will go away. Keeping our heads down and our mouths shut has provided the institution with tacit permission and now we've been unchurched!
- No more will we "CUT AND RUN" to some supposedly better place. Leaving in silence leaves the agendas unnamed and silently acquiesces to those who have thrust division upon us.
- We will "STAND AND CONFESS!" that we have been unchurched by the ELCA's slide through heresy, into schism, and landing in apostasy!

Confession and Historic Perils

The writing of this treatise was undertaken with fear and trembling. Who wants to oppose the powerful and mighty? The institutional structure of the ELCA with its control over the rostering and mobility of pastors can bring an immense amount of pressure to conform upon its rostered leaders. Only a slip of paper stands between me and the ELCA's institutional might: my letter of call to be pastor at Wilmington and Trinity Lutheran Churches.

The responsibility laid upon me by my ordination vows (see Appendix III) requires me to preach and teach in accordance with the Word of God, the Holy Scriptures, the Lutheran Confessions, and the Confession of Faith of my church. Preaching and teaching in accordance with those vows demands that I: 1) oppose the various legislative initiatives of the ELCA as — by one decision after another — my church "unchurched" me; and, 2) keep the congregations which called me to be their preacher and teacher aware of the ELCA's constitutional violations. I have already confessed the failure of my opposition and my informing.

Luther knew all too well the truth of the matter: where ever the Gospel is preached in its sweet purity, there the forces of the "unholy trinity" — the devil, the world, and the power of the flesh — are brought to bear in order to silence it. And so through the years I've come to know — anecdotally, to be sure... for who keeps statistics on these things — of the persecutions, troubles, trials, and afflictions heaped upon pastors by the institutional ELCA. I fully expect to be numbered among them.

When the Augsburg Confession was rejected by the Emperor Charles V in 1530, the Lutheran preachers, pastors, princes, theologians, etc who signed their names in subscription to it were the first to be "bound to confess and resist." Their standing as confessors of true faith over and against the combined might of the empire and the papacy put them at risk for losing goods, honor, spouse, and life. But sign they did.

In the 1550's, the emperor's armies over ran the Lutheran lands. Those "bound to confess and resist" did so — not just against the forces of the emperor and pope but also against the pleas of friends who thought they could have peace through compromise. During that time this "confessing" became known by its Latin name *"in statu confessionis."*

Through the centuries since, at various times those bound by their vows to preach and teach in accordance to the Word of God, Holy Scripture, and the Lutheran Confessions have declared *"in statu confessionis"* against blatant error by the church. A couple notable times[5] are when the German church colluded with the Third Reich and when the South African church enabled the practice of apartheid. *"In statu confessionis"* was declared against them. That "status" was resolved by the German's defeat in war and by the South African government relinquishing its practice of apartheid.

You will learn as you read this declaration that the ELCA's situation has little, if anything to do with "being nice" or not to homosexuals. This declaration of *"in statu confessionis"*-- (Stand and Confess!) reveals a struggle over the TRUTH itself: what is it; who will define it; and does it even exist? The struggle may already be lost in the ELCA. Be that as God wills. My declaration is for the sake of the larger struggle, the greater conflict. I declare in the hope that succeeding generations
- will have preachers who deliver Christ, and him crucified; and
- by such preaching know **Christ as THE WAY, THE TRUTH, and THE LIFE**; and

- experience their freedom in Christ within a society ordered well enough for their freedom to be enjoyed.

A CALL FOR REPENTANCE AND FAITH

Whereas

The ELCA (Evangelical Lutheran Church in America) — by its actions during the 2009 Church Wide Assembly (CWA) and by the actions of previous CWAs — has

- Made itself different *"from the historic Christian tradition and the Lutheran Confessions."*[6] It is now heretical and heterodox; and
- Ceased to be "church" as defined by Article VII of the Augsburg Confession.[7] It has "unchurched" me and all confessors;[8]
- Confused Law and Gospel. It now "binds the loosing and looses the binding;"[9]
- Changed the Sixth Commandment and altered the order of marriage, thereby denying the God who gives commandments and orders creation. It is now "Apostate" — outside of the faith handed down from the Apostles;

Therefore, I say

- to the voting members of the ELCA's 2009 CWA who voted in the affirmative for the "sexual" issues;
- to the ELCA's institutional leadership who have through the years promoted the agendas that have brought the institutional ELCA to such heterodoxy, unchurching, confusion, and apostasy;
- to the members of the ELCA — pastors and lay — who support and celebrate the success of those agendas;

YOU ARE WRONG!
REPENT AND BELIEVE!
YOUR SINS ARE FORGIVEN FOR JESUS' SAKE.
IN THE NAME OF THE FATHER, AND OF THE SON+
AND OF THE HOLY SPIRIT. AMEN

The time for talk is over. The time for confessing is at hand. Division has been thrust upon us. Throughout this treatise "we" and "us" and "membership" identify those of us who recall with loyalty the strength and uniqueness of our Lutheran tradition and the necessity of "Christ Alone!" We have had division thrust upon us and have been unchurched by the success of various agendas within the ELCA. The use of "they" and "them" and "ELCA" and "institutional" indentify the ones who have inflicted the unchurching upon us. By promoting those various agendas, they have traveled the path of heterodoxy and heresy, delivered schism, and are in apostasy.

Some Definitions

Orthodoxy-- The word orthodox is typically used to mean adhering to the accepted or traditional and established faith, especially in religion.[10]

Heterodoxy — Heterodoxy is the teaching of "any opinions or doctrines different from the official or <u>orthodox</u> position". The noun *heterodoxy* is synonymous with *unorthodoxy*.[11]

Heresy--is proposing some unorthodox change to an established system of belief, especially a religion. One who espouses heresy is called a heretic.[12]

Schism-- A schism is a split or division between people, usually belonging to an organization or movement. The word is most frequently applied to a division within some religion.[13]

Apostasy — Apostasy is the actual act of the abandonment or renunciation of one's religion. One who commits apostasy is an apostate. For a Christian apostasy means to abandon the faith handed down from the Apostles.[14]

"unchurched" — The members of the ELCA can no longer expect that it is an assembly of believers where the gospel is preached rightly and the sacraments are given in accordance with that gospel. They have been "unchurched."

The Office of the Keys
- is a power or commandment of God, to preach the Gospel, to **"LOOSE"** and **"BIND"** sins, and to administer sacraments. For with that commandment, Christ sends forth His Apostles:
- "When he had said this, he breathed on them and said to them, "Receive the Holy Spirit. If you forgive the sins of any, they are forgiven them; if you retain the sins of any, they are retained."[15]

INTRODUCTION:

INTRODUCTION

The structure of this document begins with **"Human Talk or God Talk"** — a section describing what just happened in August, how it could have happened, and considering what's happening now. The second section — **"The Path to Apostasy: Human Talk"** — tells you what has been happening for years: the ELCA's slide into heresy, schism, and apostasy; and how we — the members — have been powerless to stop it. The third section — **"The Path to Confessing: God Talk"** — lays out why we — the "unchurched" — should be making things happen, now and what should be happening. The final three sections **"Appendices"** — pages of resources helpful to understanding what's happening; **"Subscribers"** — pages left blank so you — the reader — can sign your name, confess the truth, and join me and the other subscribers *"in statu confessionis"* — (Stand and Confess!) and **"End Notes"** — pages providing the sources for information referenced in this document.

HUMAN TALK OR GOD TALK

WHAT JUST HAPPENED? This chapter reviews the official actions of the 2009 church wide assembly (CWA) of the Evangelical Church in America (ELCA) and situates those actions in the ELCA's path to apostasy.

HOW COULD IT HAPPEN? This chapter compares the "bound conscience" of the sexuality statement with Luther's conscience captured by the Word of God.

IT WAS HAPPENING BACK THEN, TOO. This chapter asks and answers a question: "Is Scripture a Wax Nose or Is It a Two-Edged Sword?" Law & Gospel are taken up with the external and internal clarity of the Word of God

WHAT'S HAPPENING NOW? names the purpose of talking points in general, sets the stage for further discussion by recounting a couple bible stories, sets forth the talking points being currently promulgated within the ELCA, and describes how they serve the institutional purposes of ELCA leadership.

THE PATH TO APOSTASY: HUMAN TALK

ABSOLUTE AUTHORITY, NO ACCOUNTABILITY
observes 1) how the ELCA came to be structured as ONE church which has three ways of expressing itself (congregations, synods, and church wide), 2) how there's been an observable, three-fold "Agenda" present since the ELCA's inception, 3) how the ELCA's structure provides for authority without

accountability, 4) how this structure "disenfranchises" the ELCA membership, and 5) how a "disenfranchised" membership is refusing to fund a politically unaccountable leadership.

THE SECOND DISENFRANCHISEMENT OF THE MEMBERSHIP The ELCA sacrifices its members' voting rights as citizens of the United States of America on the altar of its Politicized Agenda. Through its constitutionally mandated quota system, the ELCA Washington Office, and the Office of Corporate Responsibility, the ELCA promotes political causes and actions which can't help but be inimical to the political choices of wide swaths of its membership.

SACRIFICING THE LUTHERAN CONFESSIONS The ELCA sacrificed its constitution loyalty to the Lutheran Confessions on the altar of its Ecumenized Agenda. For the sake of an idolatrous goal of "visible unity" between Christian denominations, the institution ELCA has pursued an Ecumenized Agenda. In the course of this pursuit, the ELCA has violated its constitutional subscription to the Lutheran understanding of 1) the office of the ministry; 2) the "real, bodily" presence of Jesus Christ in the Lord's Supper; and 3) the freedom of the Gospel as God's "self-authenticating" Word; 4) the "article on which the church stands or falls" — justification by faith alone.

SACRIFICING THE DIVINE
The ELCA has sacrificed 1) the biblical language for God; 2) the Word of God in its creative authority; and 3) the biblical boundaries on sexual expression in order to achieve a Sexualized Agenda. The ELCA has rebelled against its creator and the creator's Word. The ELCA has asserted freedom from its creator and has bound the creator's Word to its interpretation. Instead of the Creator's Word binding its creature; the creature now binds its creator.

THE PATH TO CONFESSING: GOD TALK

SILENCE IS NOT AN OPTION!
This Chapter declares that we must confess for the sake of Gospel, for the sake of the generation yet to come, for the sake of fellow confessors, and for the sake of the truth.

WHAT SHALL WE SAY (OR DO)?
This chapter examines both confessing strategies which are preaching only — no legislating, and voting strategies which can of necessity be legislative.

APPENDICES:

This section contains useful information and resources referred to in this treatise.

SUBSCRIBERS:

This section is for fellow confessors to join me *"in statu confessionis"* by signing their name and subscribing in agreement.

END NOTES: This section contains the reference and source material information for this treatise.

HUMAN TALK

OR

GOD TALK

The time for talking has passed. The time for confessing is at hand. Division has been thrust upon us. No more time can be wasted trying to convince "hard cases."[16] Upon such hardened hearts only the Word of God can be effective. So I will declare the sweetness of the Gospel *("For I am not ashamed of the gospel, for it is God's power for salvation to everyone who believes"* Romans 1:16) into the depths of their error, announcing to them that our Lord Jesus Christ has forgiven them their sin. With that preaching of the Gospel, the Holy Spirit will "call, gather, enlighten, sanctify and keep them in the one true faith"[17] — which is Jesus Christ,

OR God will continue to harden their hearts so that they may be bound to the consequences of their sin and thereby know the wrath of God *("Therefore God gave them over in the desires of their hearts to impurity, to dishonor their bodies among themselves. They exchanged the truth of God for a lie and worshiped and served the creation rather than the Creator, who is blessed forever! Amen."* Romans 1:24-26)

WHAT JUST HAPPENED?

Well, first we should look at what happened at the church wide assembly (CWA) in August, 2009. Two documents were approved by the CWA: a social statement on human sexuality and a series of implementing resolutions that changed policy in the ELCA regarding the sexual behavior of pastors. A social statement in the ELCA functions as a teaching tool, a policy base, and a public witness for issues of importance to the ELCA.[18] This particular social statement: "Human Sexuality: Gift and Trust"[19] set forth the future teaching, rationale for policy, and the words to be used publically within and without by the ELCA. The social statement established (among other things) that the ELCA has **NO CLEAR WORD TO SAY REGARDING HOMOSEXUALITY**: some in the church think it's an acceptable behavior (even though they admit that such thinking violates the Lutheran Confessions and stands outside 2,000 years of Christian teaching)[20] and others think it's wrong. The implementing resolutions[21] do four things:

- They declare we can all get along if we just respect the "bound consciences" of others,
- They give permission for the blessing of publically accountable, life-long, monogamous, same gender relationships (PALMSGR) which some will call marriage[22]
- They commit the ELCA to allowing members in a PALMSGR to be on the clergy roster of "This Church," and
- They direct the formation of such policy as necessary to implement the first three resolutions in a manner that respects the "bound consciences" of all.

Contrary to the talking points used to promote and defend the CWA's votes, the issue of endorsing homosexual behavior is **NOT** the main concern for voices raised in opposition to the decisions of the CWA in August, 2009. The endorsement of homosexual behavior is a concern, yes, but it is only one presenting symptom of problems present in the ELCA from its inception. From the beginning and consistently throughout its history the ELCA has made erroneous major decisions. These decisions can be categorized into three types:

- 1) A Politicized Agenda;
- 2) An Ecumenized Agenda; and
- 3) A Sexualized Agenda.

These decisions have exposed a "schism" — a divide — within the ELCA. On one side are those of us who remember with loyalty the strength and uniqueness of our Lutheran tradition and the necessity of "Christ Alone!" We have had division thrust upon us. On the other side are those responsible for the schism. They have vocally and vigorously supported the agendas and achieved their success. They have brought a time of decision and confessing upon the ELCA.

With such voices behind them, the ELCA leadership has proved incapable of recanting or reforming its agenda-driven decisions. The time for exposure has arrived. This treatise exposes the consequences of the ELCA's decisions:

- A Politicized Agenda whose implementation has given the ELCA authority with no accountability;
- An Ecumenized Agenda which has sacrificed the Lutheran Confessions;
- A Sexualized Agenda which has sacrificed:
  - a) the biblical language for God;
  - b) the Word of God in its creative authority;
  - c) the biblical boundaries on sexual expression.

The success of these agendas has brought the ELCA down the path of heresy, worked schism upon us, and landed them in apostasy. That success has "unchurched" us. We will not be silent any longer!

HOW COULD IT HAPPEN?

The enactment of the social statement on human sexuality and the ministry proposal implementing resolutions at the CWA of 2009, could only take place in a situation wherein the ELCA has forfeited the traditional Lutheran respect for the Word of God.

Here's how that happened. The social statement appealed to something called a "bound conscience." The social statement first said that there is a difference of opinion on what the bible says regarding homosexuality. Because of that the ELCA has no clear word to say. Some can say it's appropriate. Others can disagree. The social statement acknowledges that these opinions can be so strongly held that it is as if people's consciences were "bound" to them.

The consequence of permitting such "bound consciences" in the ELCA are three-fold: 1) Those in the ELCA whose conscience is "bound" to their particular way of interpreting the bible now have permission and authority to declare homosexual behavior an acceptable lifestyle choice. 2) If such people engage in homosexual behavior themselves, and if they desire to be ordained pastors in the ELCA, then they must confine their homosexual behavior to a "publically accountable, life-long, monogamous same-gender relationship" (PALMSGR). 3) These "conscience bound" people will have a special liturgical "rite" performed for them within the ELCA — some will call this marriage.

The authors of the social statement took great care in their attempt to connect the "bound conscience" of their origination with Martin Luther's defiant stance before the Emperor at the Diet of Worms. Here's what the authors claim:

*"We understand that, in this discernment about ethics and church practice, **faithful people can and will come to different conclusions about the meaning of Scripture** and about what constitutes responsible action. We further believe that this church, on the basis of "the bound conscience," will include these different understandings and practices within its life as it seeks to live out is mission and ministry in the world."*[23]

Now read Luther's words:

Unless I am convicted by the testimony of Scripture (Jh. 8:9) or by evident reason - for I trust neither in popes nor in councils alone, since it is obvious that they have often erred (Num.15:22; Ps. 119:110; Isa.28:7; 1Tim.6: 20,21) and contradicted themselves -

*I am convicted by the Scripture which I have mentioned and **my conscience is captive by the Word of God** (2.Cor. 4:2). Therefore I cannot and will not recant, since it is difficult, unprofitable and dangerous indeed to do anything against one's conscience, (Mt. 25:30). God help me. Amen." (Isa. 50:9)*

Compare the subject and verbs in the sentences adopted by the ELCA with the subject and verbs in the sentences that Luther actually spoke.

There is an obvious difference isn't there? It is the difference between being the actor and the one acted upon. In the social statement "people" are the actors. They "understand;" they "conclude;" they derive a "meaning" of Scripture. Because of their own conclusions, understandings, and meanings, they are "bound" by their own conscience. Contrast those human works with Luther's declaration. He was **NOT** the actor; he was the one acted upon: he was passive as Scripture "convicted" him; his conscience was taken "captive" by the Word of God.

The contrast couldn't be greater! Is the "binding" of a "bound conscience" human work or God's work! There is NO WAY to equate the "bound conscience" now approved by the ELCA with Luther's conscience "captive" to the Word of God. In the comparison, the "bound conscience" of the social statement seems just like another version of Collin Raye's "That's My Story and I'm Stickin' to It." *(See Appendix XII)*

IT WAS HAPPENING BACK THEN, TOO

This contrast between Luther's declaration at Worms and the words of the social statement should not be a surprise to historically informed Lutherans. It reflects the circumstances surrounding the birth of the Reformation itself

- For Luther it is the Word of God itself which is the active agent. The Word of God — which includes its understanding as the person of Jesus Christ — has caught hold of Luther and taken him captive, replacing his conscience with the presence of Jesus Christ. Those who are shaped and normed by Scripture and the Lutheran Confessions are Luther's successors.

- For the papal party of the Reformation era it is the reader — the interpreter — who is the active agent. The reader seeks to glean some particular understanding from scripture and then — once the desired understanding is "discovered" — the interpreter declares him/herself "bound" to that understanding, replacing the Word of God in his/her conscience with their own words. The authors of the social statement and those who support it are successors to the papal party.

Scripture: A Wax Nose or a Two-Edged Sword?

At the beginning of the Reformation the papal party forced a four-fold method of interpretation upon Scripture. The interpreters looked for and found four kinds of meaning:
- Literal — what it meant to the people at the time of writing,
- Allegorical — what it means for the soul's journey to heaven,
- Anagogical — what it means for your experience in the end times, and
- Tropological — what it means for your moral life in the present.

These various means of interpretation (or as the ELCA's social statement says: various "conclusions" and various "understandings") gave the interpreter authority over Scripture. They were able to give it a "wax nose" (as Luther would put it) which could point in whatever direction best served the interpreter and the papal party.

In those days bishops were often church authorities and civil authorities. This practiced commingled and confused the two authorities. Church authority is exercised through the preaching of the Word. Civil authority is exercised through the threat of coercive force. When the two are commingled both church and civil government can tyrannize the people with threats of coercive and eternal punishment.

Into this tyranny Luther and the other Reformers preached the Good News of the GOSPEL of Jesus Christ in order to deliver the people from their bondage and set them free by faith in Christ. Preaching the Gospel clarified the two authorities, kept them in their proper place, and relieved the commingling of coercive and eternal punishment.

The people really liked this freedom from tyranny. They liked it so much that they began to consider or imagine themselves free from the normal, everyday obligations of family, community, and citizenship. They abused the freedom of their baptism. Their moral life degenerated and they – in Luther's words – "lived like pigs." Forgetting that there was a "law," they became a law unto themselves. (cf. Judges 21:25 – *"Each man did what he considered to be right."*)

To address this abuse of freedom the Reformers turned to the "external clarity" of Scripture; that is, the bible says what it means and means what it says; the bible's words are there, plain on the page, publically available for everyone to see, and these words – the Word of God – make great demands on people and how they should behave in families, communities, and as citizens.

This "external clarity" – since it was publically available – was the only "meaning" of Scripture which could be used as a basis for public policy. This "external clarity" is God's FIRST USE OF THE LAW upon his creatures. God uses the LAW to order our lives so that – even if we "conclude" differently – we will have the LAW spoken to us as an "external" word. God doesn't want us to look to ourselves and deliver our "private" interpretations. He wants to "tell" us the LAW by his Word.

Because God's Word can be so demanding, the Reformers were very careful about which ones and how many of them they enacted into policy either as church rules or civil government. They understood that "legislative" action by either church or state was a coercive "power of the sword." Commingling the authority of God's Word with the power of the sword came reluctantly to them.

The Reformers did not stop at confessing the Word's "external clarity, "for they confessed an "internal clarity" as well; that is, the scriptures interpret themselves. More pointedly, the scriptures do the interpreting themselves. The Scriptures are the Word of God — a living and active Word accomplishing the purpose for which God sends it forth. The Scriptures go to work on the reader (hearer or interpreter) bring the reader to an "internal clarity" regarding himself. This "internal clarity" is GOD'S SECOND USE OF THE LAW.

Now "clarified" by God's Law in its second use, the reader realizes that the tables have been turned. He is no longer the acting subject of the sentence; he has become the one acted upon. The reader has just been "read." The "interpreter" has just been "interpreted." He is now convicted of the truth about himself and God: He is a mortal sinner, dead in sin, and his only life is the life of God's Son Jesus Christ. This internal clarity drives one deep into the Word of God; it takes one "captive." In that bondage the Word brings to fruition the humility of John the Baptist's words: "He must increase and I must decrease." The humiliation continues until all that remains is Jesus himself — as Paul declares in Galatians 2:20: *"It is no longer I who live but Christ who lives in me."* Here, in the depths of truth, the Word of God is no longer LAW but GOSPEL. Here, in the mystery of faith, Jesus Christ swallows up the LAW. *"Christ is the end of the law for all who believe."* (Romans 10:4)

Out of death (the condemnation of the Law) has come life (the promise of Christ in the Gospel). This new person — this "saint" — is a captive, conscience and all, to the Word of God, Jesus Christ. Such a one can't help but speak the truth about himself and God. Such a one bursts forth from the tomb of sin, from slavery to the Law, and preaches Christ. This one can't wait to declare freedom in the face of tyranny — to preach Christ and his freedom. *"Come, see a man who told me all the things that I have done; this is not the Christ, is it?"* (John 4:29)

Right at this point, when they should have been "captive" in the depths of truth, the voters of the CWA turned to a lie. If their conscience truly had been "bound" by the Word of God, they would have refused to "legislate." They would have not returned themselves to the tyranny of the law. They would have burst forth from the assembly as preachers!

Alas, their consciences were not captive to the Word of God. Instead their "bound conscience" was captive to their own "concludings" and "understandings." They surrendered the authority of the Gospel and abdicated the Office of Keys. They refused to exercise their God-given authority to bind and loose sins by declaring the Word of God as Law and Gospel. They presumed to exercise their human-derived authority and "legislated" sin away. **"The assembly has effectively bound the loosing and loosed the binding."**[24]

They failed to heed Paul's admonition to the Galatians: *"Stand fast therefore in the liberty with which Christ has made us free, and be not entangled again with the yoke of bondage."* (Galatians 5:1, AKJV)

That is how it came to pass. The Lutheran respect for the "external" and "internal" clarity of Scripture as the living and active Word of God was rejected by the 2009 CWA. The CWA chose the "wax nose" of their own bondage. In the hardness of their hearts they rejected the "two-edged sword" of Law and Gospel which would have sliced through their bondage, captivated them with its truth, and — having bound them to Jesus — set them free. By majority vote the members expressed their own personal desires. Because the CWA is the "highest legislative authority" of This Church, those personal desires are now binding on the operation of the ELCA.

WHAT'S HAPPENING NOW?

THE USEFULNESS OF TALKING POINTS

Now that the CWA has acted and exposed the institutional ELCA as heretical, schismatic, and apostate, the leadership of the church wide and synodical organizations are busily promoting a series of talking points in a frantic effort to restore the membership's complacency. We've all become familiar with the concept of talking points: Talking points are a series of statements meant to define or "frame" an issue in a way that benefits their originator. Talking points may or may not reflect the "truth" of the issue or situation; but as they are repeated loud enough and long enough, they come to be perceived by their hearers as the truth of the issue or situation.

The development of talking points and their being repeated loud enough and long enough has been one of the most successful strategies used by the institutional ELCA. Talking points reassured the membership, keeping it complacent. Meanwhile — at the church wide organization and at church wide assemblies — the ELCA constitution and its confession of faith were being violated. Decision by decision the three agendas have been implemented. A variety of favorable talking points have prepared their way.

TWO BIBLICAL CONVERSATIONS

This brings to mind a couple biblical conversations — one general and ongoing across some centuries and the other very particular, pointed and brief. The first was the generations-long conversation — perhaps "conflict" would be more appropriate — between the "tame" prophets and the "wild" prophets in ancient Israel and Judah. The second was the interrogation Pontius Pilate put Jesus through prior to handing him over to be crucified.

When the biblical prophets burst onto the scene, there were two camps — "wild" prophets and "tame" prophets — each claiming to speak "the Word of the Lord." The "wild" prophets were the men who came from the margins, from the wilderness, from the everyday occupations of regular people. The "tame" prophets were the men who frequented the royal courts, the temple precincts; they were the children of wealth and influence, favored by kings and high priests alike.[25]

The one who pays the piper gets to call the tune!

The prophetic camps declared opposing messages as the "Word of the Lord." One camp declared judgment upon the actions of the kings and rulers. The other camp ratified the actions of those same kings and rulers. The people had to discern which prophets truly spoke "the Word of the Lord." To discern the truth they asked themselves "Who benefits?" [26]

The one who pays the piper gets to call the tune.

The obviousness of the situation was hard to miss: the "tame" prophets stood to keep or advance their positions and benefits as members of the royal court and temple precincts. The "wild" prophets stood to lose not just their freedom but perhaps their heads as well (Recall the demise of John the Baptist? Matthew 14:9-11). Those "wild" prophets challenged the rich, royal, and powerful in the use of their wealth and influence to redefine the truth!

The one who pays the piper gets to call the tune.

History has ratified the "wild" prophets and acknowledged the truth of their speaking "the Word of the Lord." Scripture includes the books of Isaiah, Jeremiah, Amos and the others while consigning those "tame" prophets to a mere mention in historical passing. *(see for example: 1 Kings 22:19-23, Isaiah 3:1-8; 28:7; Jeremiah 5:31; 13:13-14; 26:1-11; Amos :10-15; Micah 3:5-11; and Zephaniah 3:4)*

The second biblical conversation was as brief as the "prophet conflict" was long. Pontius Pilate — the Roman governor of Palestine — exchanged only a few words with Jesus. Pilate was interrogating Jesus to discover whether or not Jesus was a "king" and therefore either a competitor or an imposter. Jesus gave him this answer:

"You say that I am a king. For this I was born, and for this I came into the world, to testify to the truth. Everyone who belongs to the truth listens to my voice." (John 18:37)

Jesus refuses to claim kingship and compete with Pilate for power; Jesus works in truth, not power. So, how does Pilate respond? He responds with a question, a question quite revealing about his attitude toward the truth: He says, "What is truth?" Could we have expected any different response from one who had the power, wealth, and influence to redefine the truth in whichever way best served his interests?

(Begin Joke) I heard that the Congressional Office of Management and Budget was looking to hire a new accountant. Ole applied. He was standing in a line of interviewees when the man in charge came down the line. He held in his hand a paper and asked each applicant to read it and give him an answer. After each applicant did so, the man shook his head and dismissed them. He got to Ole. Ole took the paper and found on it a column of figures and heard the man asking him what the total was. Remembering how the others had been dismissed, Ole looked at the man in charge and answered, "What would you like the total to be?" Ole got the job. *(End Joke)*

So it is with religious institutions as well: those in charge take authoritative texts, turn to their tame theologians for interpretation, and ask: "What does this mean?" The theologians, knowing full well that "He who pays the piper calls the tune," answer them, "What do you want it to mean?"

In the kingdoms of this world — even the "religious" kingdoms established beneath and within the brokenness of sin — power is nothing less than the ability to define truth; and then wield that redefined truth in service of the institution's own interests and benefit.

THE CONVERSATION TODAY

The conversation in the ELCA today is dominated by a series of "talking points" promulgated by the institution's leadership, designed to minimize ELCA members' response to the apostate actions of the 2009 CWA, and to restore the members to complacency.

Anyone who's been paying attention at all in these days following the assembly will have heard statements like these:

- "The people who made this decision are just like you!"
- "Let's stay in conversation." "Let's not stop talking." "I want to hear your story, listen to your concerns, feel your pain."
- "Nothing's going to change: You'll still be able to do as you please in your congregation."
- "We're just going to be going down two parallel tracks now — separate but equal."
- "What's the matter? Don't you want to be nice to homosexuals?"
- "Doesn't the bible address other sins that are more important, like poverty and feeding the hungry?"

- "Don't redirect your benevolence, just think of all the "good" programs you'll be hurting."

That's an excellent list of talking points: not too long, not too short; easy to keep track of, they reinforce each other, and are very effective upon us, the membership of the ELCA. You who recall with loyalty the strength and uniqueness of our Lutheran tradition have several qualities that make you some of the finest people in the world and I rejoice that the Holy Spirit has called me to a parish full of them.

The qualities you possess are:

- A desire to be "nice" people and good neighbors;
- A desire to avoid confrontation and conflict;
- A desire to think and speak well of their leaders.

These are admirable qualities. They make the members of "my church" easy and fun to be around and to have as neighbors. These qualities also ease the imposition of agendas upon them. Let's take a look at each of the talking points and see how it plays to those admirable qualities.

"The people who made this decision are just like you!" Oh, really? The last time I looked no congregation was made up of forty percent clergy (a quota established for the CWA in the constitution). The people in my community are all accountable to someone for their actions, unlike the members of the CWA. The people in my community have to experience the consequences of their decisions, unlike the members of the CWA. The members of my community know they are part of a history and tradition, and that they bear responsibility to and for that history and tradition – unlike the CWA which has no past or any future. The people in my community make their decisions in the context of their immediate neighbors, not isolated from home, family, and community like the members of the CWA. The people who made this decision at the CWA ARE NOT like you at all!

"Let's stay in conversation." To hear the ELCA leadership speak, you'd think the biggest sin in the church right now is to stop talking. This plays very well to the members who want to be nice people and good neighbors, avoiding confrontation and conflict. Such people have experienced firsthand the reality of ongoing conflict and broken relationships between neighbors when one says to the other: "I'm not going to talk to you anymore!" In close knit

communities where neighbors must depend on neighbors, this is a serious consequence of conflict. Of course, it plays very well for the purposes of the ELCA leadership. They know that talk is a substitute for action: as long as people are "talking," they're less likely to be "doing" — as in taking action to redirect benevolence, organize with others, or take a vote to leave. They know, too, that "time heals all wounds," and that the more time passes, the immediacy of the offense is lessened and people lose the imperative to "do" something.

"Nothing's going to change." This plays well to the membership since people tend to focus on the life of their own congregation. It gives them a reason to avoid confrontation and conflict if their own congregation doesn't "have" to change. This plays well to the leadership's agenda, too. By keeping the members focused on their own congregations, they won't notice the radical alterations going on at the church wide and synod levels of the ELCA

"We're just going down two separate, parallel tracks." Being nice people and good neighbors, ELCA members are attracted to the idea of "live and let live." When they hear this language, right away an image forms for them: that of a pair of railroad tracks disappearing in tandem over the horizon. It's a comfortable image and one easy to live with. But, as much as leadership promotes this image, it is far from reality. By their own admission in adopting the social statement, the voting members of the CWA set the ELCA on a widely divergent course from historical Christianity and the Lutheran Confessions. Because they have rejected the constraints of tradition and broken out of the biblical boundaries, a more appropriate image for what they have done is that of a "fork in the road — one goes this way and the other, that."

"What's the matter? Don't you want to be nice to homosexuals?" This one plays right into the memberships' sense of guilt. In today's world we are at the most only one neighbor away from being connected personally to someone who prefers homosexual behavior. Most often we know of such people as "nice," maybe even as good community members. The membership does not want to think ill of such people nor do they want others to have even a remote opportunity to consider that they might be "homophobic bigots."   So, in the face of the accusation — concerned and a little guilty that someone might think it true — the membership goes quiet and doesn't raise any objections.

"Doesn't the bible address other sins that are more important, like poverty and feeding the hungry?" Well, yes, the bible does have some clear things to say about poverty, etc. The membership knows this and will feel again a stab of guilt over how they personally try to help the poor and hungry. But equating the various biblical sins is not the issue and the leadership knows this. The issue is the schismatic actions promoted by the leadership and ratified by the CWA.

"Don't redirect your benevolence, just think of all the "good" programs you'll be hurting." Stories of people in need — especially if there's a face or family attached to the stories for the membership to connect with — these stories stir up emotions. The people are being enticed into handing over their inheritance in the Christian tradition for the price of giving a bowl of soup for the hungry. There are a myriad of "good" programs helping people and never enough money for them. Just because benevolence dollars are not flowing into the ELCA's coffers, doesn't mean that the people redirecting benevolence have stopped helping others.

The talking points allow the ELCA leadership to play to the special qualities of its membership so that the leadership can reframe and redefine the issue by repeating those talking points loud enough and long enough. Like the patter of a capable stage magician, the talking points direct the members' attention away from the hand where the "real" action is taking place: the violation of the ELCA's own Confession of Faith and the abandonment of the Christian tradition.

As You Pray, So You Believe

I need to interrupt here for a moment. The significance of establishing a liturgical ceremony for blessing a PALMSGR — which some will call marriage — must not escape notice. A well-known principle among religions is this one: *"lex orandi, lex credenda"* — "the law of prayer is the law of belief." [27]

Prayer and liturgy are inseparable. They are the most frequent of our religious activities. The evidence of history demonstrates time and again that the most effective way to change people's belief is to change the words of their liturgies and prayers.

Our worship and our prayers are how we "talk" with God. The words we use are our "talking points." When we are given "new" and "different" talking points that become repeated long enough and loud enough through our prayers and liturgies, soon we come to accept and promote them as proper belief.

One of the most effective and persistent "talking points" used by the ELCA to bring about the success of its agendas has been this: "You just have to do it; you don't have to believe it."[28] Time and again we have been reassured that this issue is not a "matter of faith," it's just another way of doing things.

They know well the maxim: *"lex orandi, lex credenda."* Asking only to exercise the law of prayer, the ELCA can wait for belief to follow. They have had time on their side. But no more! The schism has been exposed. The time for division has been thrust upon us. It's time to confess!

THE

PATH

TO

APOSTASY:

HUMAN TALK

The writing of this treatise was undertaken with fear and trembling. Who wants to oppose the powerful and mighty? The institutional structure of the ELCA with its control over the rostering and mobility of pastors can bring an immense amount of pressure to conform upon its rostered leaders. Only a slip of paper stands between me and the ELCA's institutional might: my letter of call to be pastor at Wilmington and Trinity Lutheran Churches. The responsibility laid upon me by my ordination vows (see Appendix III) requires me to preach and teach in accordance with the Word of God, the Holy Scriptures, the Lutheran Confessions, and the Confession of Faith of my church. Fulfilling those vows meant opposing the various legislative initiatives of the ELCA as—by one decision after another—my church reached this despicable place and by keeping the congregations which called me to be their preacher aware of the ELCA's constitutional violations. I have already confessed the failure of my opposition.

ABSOLUTE AUTHORITY, NO ACCOUNTIBILITY

A New Way of "Being" Church

In its constituting documents the ELCA proposed (and enacted) a different way of being church than is usual among Lutherans and other Protestants. The usual thinking reflected this process: At the "grass-roots" Lutherans banded together in congregations, and congregations banded together into organizations called denominations or sometimes "churches." The ELCA constitution "thought" differently. There was to be only the single entity calling itself "This Church." This Church has three expressions: congregations, synods, and church wide. In previous Lutheran denominations the various levels of "organization," (e.g. congregation, synod, denomination) were ways of organizing the "grass roots." In the ELCA this understanding was reversed. The ELCA's three expressions are the "way" the one single entity of "This Church" is organized. The usual way of thinking considered "organization" a bottom-up affair. ELCA thinking turned that upside down. In the ELCA organization is a top down affair. Such an understanding is unfamiliar to most Lutherans and Protestants but widely understood in Episcopal, Roman, and Orthodox churches. While this way of thinking has not influenced the operation of most congregations or entered the thinking of most members, it has enabled the authoritarian behavior of the church wide expression and many synods.

The "AGENDA" of the New Church, the ELCA

A historical retrospective on the formation of the ELCA and its subsequent behavior can observe that its actions — whatever the motives behind them — can be categorized by the word "AGENDA;" that is, the actions and decisions observably accomplish something whether that "something" was intentional or not.

The AGENDA advanced by those decisions has, observably, abandoned much that is familiar and traditional while establishing much that is new, innovative, and unfamiliar. The ELCA's actions and decisions — the success of its AGENDA — can be divided into

- A Politicized Agenda: Establishing the ELCA as an agent of "social change;"

- An Ecumenized Agenda: Achieving "visible unity" among the Christian denominations of the world; and,
- A Sexualized Agenda: Removing all vestiges of "so-called" patriarchal oppression by loosening the biblical constraints on language and sexual expression.

The success of these agendas has sacrificed much that you and I trust as familiar and traditional. They've sacrificed what you and I have thought is a given—adherence to the ELCA's confession of faith. (See Appendix II) Success for the Politicized Agenda has sacrificed the enfranchisement (voting rights) of the ELCA's members. Success for the Ecumenized Agenda has sacrificed the Lutheran Confessions. Success for the Sexualized Agenda has sacrificed 1) the biblical language for God, 2) the Word of God in its creative authority, and 3) the biblical boundaries on sexual expression. Taken together, the success of these Agendas has resulted in the ELCA violating its own constitutional confession of faith, set it down a schismatic course, and delivered it into apostasy—it no longer has the faith handed down from the apostles.

THE **FIRST** DISENFRANCHISEMENT OF **ELCA** MEMBERS

Most ELCA members transfer their experience as citizens within their communities and as members of other democratic organizations into their experience of the ELCA. That previous experience misinforms them. The ELCA is **NOT** a representative democracy. Local congregations may still function that way but there is no requirement that they do so. For the ELCA each expression of "This Church" has a body which is its "highest legislative authority." The congregation has its annual meeting of voting members; the synod has its annual Synod Assembly of voting members; and church wide has its biennial Church Wide Assembly of voting members.

Congregations usually elect (or appoint) people from their midst to be voting members to their synod's assembly. Synods usually elect (or appoint) people from their midst to be voting members to the bi-annual church wide assembly. These voting members are **NOT** delegates or representatives. They are specifically admonished to remember that their authority to act is not "delegated" to them by the body that elected them and that they have **NO** responsibility to represent the body that elected them. They are told that, as they meet in synod assembly or church wide assembly, they — and **THEY ALONE** — constitute that "expression" of "This Church."

These assemblies of voting members exist only for the time they are present with one another. They have **NO** "past" memories to provide them with continuity. They have **NO** anticipation of "future" consequences to which they will be held accountable. They have only their personal desires and the opportunity to gratify them in secret by casting an anonymous ballot. The majority of those personal desires becomes the binding decision of that syndical or church wide "expression" of the church at that moment.

There is **NO** roll call record of how voting members voted on any specific issue. Voting members have **NO** responsibility to report back to the body that elected them regarding how they voted. **NO** decision of the synod assembly can be referred to its member congregations for ratification or rejection. **NO** decision of the church wide assembly can be referred to its member congregations or member synods for ratification or rejection. There is **NO** mechanism within the structure of the This Church by which the members of the ELCA can hold synod assemblies or church wide assemblies accountable for their actions. Though leadership is "elected" by assemblies, each assembly is a unique event. It has **NO** past and **NO** future. The individual members of the ELCA have **NO** political means to hold the elected leaders of "This Church" accountable for their actions.

Simply put, the ELCA as "This Church" is a collective of 65 synodical centers of power and authority overseen by the church wide center of power and authority. All 66 of these "royal courts" exercise their authority without any political means of holding them accountable for the decisions they make. There are **NO** checks and balances within the ELCA. It was designed that way. Whether intentional or not, the ELCA's constitutional structure has served to both disenfranchise its membership and enable the decisions characterized as its AGENDA.

Even when the actions and decisions within that AGENDA result in violations of its own constitution and its confession of faith, the members of the ELCA have **NO** authority to which appeal can be made; **NO** adjudicative body that can weigh the violation and issue a determination. There is no independent prosecutor, judge, or jury to rule on its actions. In consequence, then, the successive CWAs have enacted measures in violation of both constitution and confession with impunity. The membership has no political or judicial means of recourse.

However, if dollars were votes, a majority would have voted the ELCA out of "power" by now. At its beginning in 1989 the church wide expression of the ELCA had received roughly 66 million dollars of benevolence money from its congregational expressions. Today, the church wide expression of the ELCA is experiencing a dramatic "short fall" in its income. Budget cuts, layoffs, and program reductions are being announced with regularity. (No wonder the people are being "talked" into keeping the money coming.) Church wide will probably end the year 2009 with about 50 million dollars of income.

If you compare incomes for 1989 and 2009, adjusting for inflation, that starting 66 million would be the equivalent of 117 million dollars in 2009. 50 divided by 117 equals 43%. Fifty-seven percent of the membership's support for the ELCA's church wide expression has eroded during the time of its actions and decisions in the Politicized, Ecumenized, and Sexualized Agendas. That lack of support is even greater when you factor in the inflation adjusted increase in income for congregations: income in congregations has grown; but those congregations' support of church wide has diminished.

The members of the ELCA are holding the church wide expression accountable in the only way available to them: they're refusing to feed an otherwise unaccountable authority. They're censoring an authority that has disenfranchised them from the beginning.

THE SECOND DISENFRANCHISEMENT OF ELCA MEMBERS

The right of the ELCA's membership to make their own political choices has been sacrificed at the altar of the Politicized Agenda. Through its success the ELCA has been established as an "agent of social change" and has been given a prophetic voice so it can "speak to truth to power."

But, this "establishing" and "giving" to the ELCA has severely compromised — sacrificed, you might say — the rights of its membership to vote for and financially support the political causes of their choice. Several means compromise the memberships political choices. Three of them — each also as unaccountable to the membership as the ELCA's church wide expression — will be exposed in their service to the Politicized Agenda and the disenfranchisement of ELCA members:

- The quota system enshrined in the ELCA constitution demands the inclusion of a fixed percentage of minorities in all decision making bodies;
- The ELCA Washington Office — the ELCA's advocacy/political influence branch in Washington, DC; and
- The Office of Corporate Responsibility which watches over the behavior of large corporations, judges them according to standards set by the ELCA, joins with other activist groups, and applies pressure — financial, political, and corporate — to align corporate behavior with the ELCA's Politicized Agenda.

The Quota System

The ELCA's mandated Quota System compromises our political rights by functioning as a form of affirmative action within the church wide organization. Like all forms of affirmative action, it has consequences both positive and negative. The positive consequences have been well announced and argued, so the negative ones will be raised here.

To start with the simplest negative consequence of legislated "inclusion" is that equal and opposite "exclusion" accompanies such legislation but is not acknowledged. This mandated exclusion provides a convenient method for replacing "wild" prophets with "tame" prophets whose voice is more acceptable to the powerful. A quota system compromises the transparency of the political process.

The reaction of those who now find themselves suddenly "included," seemingly at the whim of the decision-makers, may well include gratitude, loyalty, and an ongoing desire to "please" those who chose them. A quota system compromises the honesty of the political process.

Another consequence of mandated inclusive choices is that "minority status" supersedes "quality control" in the selection of participants. The one most qualified is not necessarily chosen for participation, but the one who meets some "quota" requirement is preferred. A quota system compromises the integrity of the political process.

The ELCA Washington Office

The ELCA Washington Office presents the ELCA as an agent of social change in the center of our nation's highest civil authority and power. There, "speaking what it has determined as truth to power," this ELCA office compromises our right to vote for and financially support political causes of our own choosing.

Read the following direct quote from its web page at www.elca.org

The ELCA Washington Office...[29]
- *Witnesses for social justice on domestic and foreign policy issues facing the nation.*
- *Represents the Evangelical Lutheran Church in America's positions within the area of public debate.*
- *Educates, informs and enables effective interaction between the Evangelical Lutheran Church in America (ELCA) and the federal government.*

Mission and work
Faithful to God's call, the ELCA Washington Office fulfills the Evangelical Lutheran Church in America's witness for social justice on domestic and foreign policy issues facing the nation, and through it, the world. With a commitment to a prophetic vision which stands with the poor and the powerless, the office represents the church's positions within the complex arena of public debate. To achieve effective interaction between the whole church and the federal government, the office educates, informs and enables full involvement of the church in this ministry.

Did you find the words: "social justice" or "prophetic vision?" Of course you did. Now recall when you made the choice to send those social justice advocates or prophetic visionaries to speak for you? Did you get to select from a slate of candidates? Did you get to give them the words to say on your behalf or your positions to represent before the powerful? Of course, you can't remember any of that because you've been disenfranchised from those political causes.

The Office of Corporate Responsibility

The Office of Corporate Responsibility which watches over the behavior of large corporations, judges them according to standards set by the ELCA, joins with other activist groups, and applies pressure — financial, political, and corporate (via annual stockholder meetings) — to align corporate behavior with the ELCA's Politicized Agenda. The following paragraphs are quotes from the www.elca.org. [30]

The Corporate Social Responsibility program operates on the belief that God's business involves all of life and that God calls the Church both corporately and individually to use all that is committed to its care to practice good stewardship of the creation (Genesis 1:26), pursue justice (Amos 5:24), care for people in need (Matthew 25:40), and seek things that make for peace (Luke 19:41-42). The Corporate Social Responsibility program seeks to dialogue with business representatives on the social implications of company practices and to affect ELCA investment policy in socially responsible ways

The Corporate Social Responsibility Program (CSR) of the Evangelical Lutheran Church in America (ELCA) is mandated by the ELCA Constitution:
Chapter 14.
CHURCH COUNCIL
14.21.14 The Church Council, acting through the designated churchwide unit, shall have responsibility for the corporate social responsibility of this church and shall have the authority to file shareholder resolutions and cast proxy ballots thereon on stocks held by the churchwide units that are not separately incorporated. In addition, the Church Council may make recommendations to the churchwide units that are separately incorporated concerning the filing of shareholder resolutions and the casting of ballots on stocks held by those units.
(08-07) ELCA CONSTITUTION – CHAPTER 14 / 101

Chapter 16.
PROGRAM UNITS OF THE CHURCHWIDE ORGANIZATION
16.12.D06. Church in Society Unit
The Church in Society unit shall assist this church to discern, understand, and respond to the needs of human beings, communities, society, and the whole creation through

direct human services and through addressing systems, structures, and policies of society, seeking to promote justice, peace, and the care of the earth. To fulfill these responsibilities, this program unit shall:

i. give expression to this church's concern for corporate social responsibility, both in its internal affairs and its interaction in the broader society. To do so, this program unit will:

1) exercise, at the direction of the Church Council, the rights of this church as a corporate shareholder on issues of social concern on stocks held by the churchwide units that are not separately incorporated. In addition, the Church Council may make recommendations to the churchwide units that are separately incorporated concerning the filing of shareholder resolutions and the casting of proxy ballots on stocks held by those units;

2) facilitate the formation of an Advisory Committee on Corporate Social Responsibility that will include representatives from the Board of Pensions, the Church Council, and other units of this church and that will give counsel and advice to all appropriate units of this church on corporate social responsibility; and

3) work with national ecumenical groups on issues of corporate responsibility.

(08-07) ELCA CONSTITUTION – CHAPTER 16 / 121

The ELCA engages with a variety of "partners" in this endeavor. (See Appendix XII for a list) The Office of Corporate Responsibility wields the financial resources and the membership numbers of the ELCA, its related organizations, and its various "partners" as its means exercising political power and influence within the corporate world. The words above demonstrate how the success of the Politicized Agenda in establishing the ELCA as an agent of social change and in giving it a so-called "prophetic" voice, has severely compromised the rights of the ELCA's membership to vote for and financially support the political causes of their choice. The Politicized Agenda has disenfranchised us politically and financially.

SACRIFICING THE LUTHERAN CONFESSIONS

The ELCA sacrificed its constitutionally-mandated loyalty to the Lutheran Confessions on the altar of its Ecumenized Agenda. Through this on-going drama, the ELCA sacrifices:

- The Lutheran Confessional enjoyment of the "single" office of ministry;
- The Lutheran Confessional insistence on the "bodily" presence of Jesus Christ in the Lord's Supper; and,
- The Lutheran Confessional insistence on the freedom of the Gospel as God's self-authenticating Word.
- The Lutheran Confessional insistence on "Justification by Faith alone" as the article upon which the church stands or falls.

THE "ORIGIN" AND "ERRORS" OF THE ECUMENICAL AGENDA

As the Commission for a New Lutheran Church (CNLC) was doing its work during the 1980's, the World Council of Churches was working toward a goal of "visible unity." Read here its established purpose:

"The primary purpose of the fellowship of churches in the World Council of Churches is to call one another to visible unity in one faith and in one Eucharistic fellowship..."[31]

The "blueprint" for achieving this visible unity was a document entitled BAPTISM, EUCHARIST, AND MINISTRY (BEM) — the "most widely-distributed and studied ecumenical document."[32] The purpose intended by the World Council of Churches as it promoted and worked to achieve the goal of visible unity is also stated in the governing documents of the WCC:[33]

"...to advance towards that unity in order that the world may believe."

BEM contained assumptions for achieving the visible unity of various Christian churches through a common understanding and practice of their sacramental life, i.e. Baptism and "Eucharist," and through the common recognition of the "three-fold order" of ministry, i.e. Bishops, presbyters and deacons.

The ELCA likewise has a constitutionally mandated (4.02f)[34] "Ecumenical Vision" established *"to manifest [make visible] the unity given to the people of God..."* This vision of visible unity is attained whenever 'full communion" is declared between the ELCA and another Christian denomination.[35] The same document includes these three points (among others) that are essential to "full communion":

- A sharing of the Lord's Supper,
- A mutual recognition and availability of ordained ministers,
- A mutual lifting of any condemnations.

Do you notice the similarity with the WCC blueprint? Full communion for the ELCA includes a common "sacramental life" and a "common recognition of ministry" just like the assumptions of BEM.

While it is certainly important to "get along" with other Christian denominations, the Ecumenized Agenda of the ELCA places a higher priority on "full communion" than on abiding by its own constitution's confession of faith. It has repeatedly violated the boundaries established by Scripture and the Lutheran Confessions for Lutheran ecumenism. Those boundaries are a "hedge of protection" summarized clearly by these necessary Christian assertions:

- Christ Alone! Jesus is exclusively "the way, the truth, and the life." Whatever is NOT Christ is not the way, but error — is not the truth, but a lie — is not life, but death.
- Word Alone! God deals with his creature solely through His Word preached to humanity as Law and Gospel. When the Gospel is given with water, wine and bread, this together with preaching are the means of grace through which the Holy Spirit works faith *(see Appendix V)*
- Faith Alone! This faith is a work of the Holy Spirit, not the product of human emotional effort. It is "hidden" in the human heart — not "visible" to our sight — in order that our confidence rests on God's Word alone and not the visible works of our hands.

The quoted ecumenical documents themselves testify to the willingness of the Ecumenized Agenda to violate the Scriptural and Confessional boundaries. The following phrases indicate how the ELCA has strayed beyond the "hedge of protection" summarized by the above assertions:

- "community in Christ…, is the basis for unity in the Church;"[36]
- To make manifest the unity given to the people of God;
- To advance toward that [visible] unity that the world may believe;
- Article VII provides a "basis for growing into greater levels of unity" (see Appendix VII)

Like the "talking points" dealt with earlier, these phrases are statements meant to define or frame the "unity" issue in a way that benefits the Ecumenized Agenda. Their repetition loud enough and long enough has given that agenda success; but success at what cost?

"Community in Christ is the basis for unity in the Church" As a talking point it has great appeal until you realize that Christ is only the "basis" for unity, he is NOT THE UNITY itself! When Christians are one in Christ are they one in Christ or does something more have to be added? According to the Ecumenized Agenda something must be added to Christ—some human work perhaps—for unity. This "talking point" contradicts the "Christ Alone" hedge of protection.

"To manifest [make visible] the unity given to the people of God" This talking point gives ecumenists a lot to do. Too bad it's already been done for them. God has taken care of it by his Word. But ecumenists are sinners just like the rest of us and have difficulty being satisfied with the Word Alone. They demand their right to add something to that Word—something like the "legislation" of full communion, for example. What the Gospel has already given them for free they want to bind up again in the Law.

"To advance toward that [visible] unity that the world may believe" Now here's a talking point full of pride! The Ecumenized Agenda assumes it can do better than the Holy Spirit. When Article V of the Augsburg Confession establishes Word and Sacrament as the Means by which the Holy Spirit works faith, it excludes any other human work. The ecumenists build careers and reputations on substituting their work—"visible unity"—in place of the work of the Holy Spirit "that the world may believe."

"Article VII provides a "basis for growing into greater levels of unity" This talking point has been popularized as "the confessions aren't a ceiling, they're a floor." A "ceiling" puts a limit on just how high the ecumenists can "pile it up." No wonder they'd rather have a floor than a ceiling. When Article VII of the Augsburg Confession declares: "it is sufficient..." (See Appendix V), it's not saying "start here and pile it up." No, the Article sets a limit. Just like Jesus Christ IS the church's unity, not its basis for unity, "it is sufficient" means the Gospel rightly preached and the sacraments rightly given ARE the unity of the Church because through them Jesus Christ is delivered.

Article VII makes quite clear and simple the Lutheran ecumenical criteria. We only have to ask two questions: Is the Gospel being preached purely? Are the sacraments being handed over in accordance with the purely preached Gospel? Scripture and Lutheran Confessions provide the discernment necessary to answer those questions. Any Christian denomination who can answer "yes" to those questions resides within the unity of the church; and that unity is revealed (made manifest) on any occasion when the gospel is preached purely.

By its own admission, the problem for the Ecumenized Agenda is that the Word of God whereby Jesus Christ is delivered and the Holy Spirit works faith is NOT enough. It is **NOT** sufficient. The Ecumenized Agenda must add something in addition to Christ. So the sacrifices are made: the single order of ministry, the Lutheran Confessions, the "real and bodily" presence of Jesus Christ, and justification by faith alone get "offered" up on ecumenism's altar.

SACRIFICING THE MINISTRY

The Ecumenized Agenda of the ELCA tried three times to change the Lutheran office of ministry into the "three-fold order" of Bishop, presbyter, and deacon. It failed twice before the successful passage of Called to Common Mission by the 1999 CWA.

To better understand this situation, one should know that the confessional Lutheran "single" order of ministry (see Appendix VI) is neither Protestant nor Catholic in its understanding of "clergy."

The Protestant tradition understands
- The clergy to be persons filling the pastor's position and exercising the authority delegated to them by the congregation.
- The clergy have no "spiritual" authority beyond that of any baptized Christian.
- Their first loyalty is to the people who elected them to the position.
- Their "call" is tantamount to being hired.

The Catholic (also the Episcopal, Anglican, and Orthodox) — the "three-fold order of Bishop, presbyter, deacon" — this tradition understands

- The clergy to be persons filling the deacon's, priests, and Bishop's position by virtue of being sent by the "church" and "ordained" into their office.
- Their ordination confers a special grace upon them — a spiritual authority which the baptized do not possess — which forever changes their character as persons. Each ordination in a "higher" spiritual office confers more grace and spiritual authority to their character. The process by which this character is passed from generation to generation is called the "Historic Episcopate;" (See Appendix VIII) that is, each successive generation receives grace and spiritual authority through the tactile transmission of the laying on of hands by the previous generation's possessors of the Historic Episcopate
- Their first loyalty is to the "church" which ordained them.
- Their "call" is an assignment from the "church."

In contrast the Lutheran tradition understands its clergy

- To have NO spiritual difference from its laity. The fullness of grace and the Holy Spirit are given entirely in baptism — nothing more needs to be added.
- All Lutheran Christians are preachers of the gospel and share in the "office of ministry". (see Appendix VI)
- Pastors are "sent out" (made available) by the church and called by the congregation.
- Once called, pastors are "ordained" — that is, the church holds a special service which recognizes and ratifies that this person is now called into the PUBLIC Office of Ministry. The pastor is now publically responsible for delivering the Means of Grace (Word and Sacrament) to the congregation(s) who has called him.
- His first loyalty is not to the congregation, nor is it to the church, but it is to the Word of God so that this Word would be declared and rightly distinguished as Law and Gospel. The pastor is a public preacher and resident theologian — a "servant" of the Word of God in order to "serve it up" to the congregation and community.

With the enactment of Called to Common Mission in 1999, the ELCA adopted the "three-fold order of ministry" acceptable to the Episcopal Church USA and inherent in the "Historic Episcopate." The Ecumenized Agenda triumphed: the Lutheran "single order" of ministry was sacrificed. The confessions were cast aside, for a victory in the ELCA's Ecumenized Agenda.

SACRIFICING THE "REAL, BODILY" PRESENCE OF JESUS

The Formula of Agreement[37] enacted at the 1997 CWA declared Full Communion with the Presbyterian Church, the Reformed Church and the United Church of Christ. Its success was overshadowed by the defeat of the Concordat. These Protestant churches are the theological descendents of John Calvin and Huldrych Zwingli who were 16th century reformers with Luther.

Both of these theologians "reasoned" that since the resurrected Jesus was sitting at the right hand of God, he couldn't really be "bodily" present in the bread and wine of Holy Communion. His presence could be there "spiritually." His presence could be there because the participants "remembered" him. But he couldn't be there bodily because that didn't make sense. Luther, however, was insistent on the "real, bodily" presence of Jesus in the bread and wine.

Luther's insistence on the "Real Presence of Christ" in the sacrament of Holy Communion was tested by controversy with Zwingli. Throughout the 1520s the two of them had kept up a running dispute over the sacrament, finally culminating in the Marburg Colloquy of 1529 as an attempt to restore a united front to the Protestant reformation. Meeting in the Marburg Castle at the behest of Philipp I of Hessen, Germany, the parties of Luther and Zwingli managed to agree on fourteen out of fifteen points of contention but could not agree on the presence of Christ in the Supper.

Zwingli said the bread and wine are merely symbols representing the body and blood of Christ. Contradicting him, Luther said the body and blood of Christ were actually given in, with, and under the bread and wine for all communicants to eat and drink. Their understanding of the nature of Christ was vastly different. Luther preached a "ubiquitous" Christ — that is, the divine AND human natures of Christ, the risen Lord, were not only together at the right hand of God but were together everywhere and at all times present. While Luther emphasized the union of Christ's two natures, Zwingli emphasized their distinction and would not agree that Christ's human body could be everywhere present even after the resurrection and even if, in his deity, he could be omnipresent. With no agreement between them, the Protestant reformation retained their differences from Lutherans and developed separate confessions of faith.

In his resistance to compromise Luther demonstrated his commitment to the "external clarity" of Scripture; that is — when Christ said "This **IS** my body" — he meant what he said and said what he meant. The words are there for anybody to see, read, and hear. Because Christ said so, his body and blood were present and real. Luther was bound by the Word of God — captivated by it. This has remained uniquely and distinctively Lutheran. Zwingli, on the other hand, "interpreted" IS as a metaphor for the word **"signifies"** and claimed there could be no real presence of Christ's body or blood because his human nature sat at the right hand of God. Zwingli was bound to his interpretation of Scripture.

Luther knew that if Jesus Christ wasn't physically, bodily, really present in the bread and wine, we'd be turned back upon ourselves. Holy Communion would not be about Jesus coming to us with his gifts; it would be about us, the participants, and how well we "remembered." Without Jesus Christ there in both his natures, divine and human, the New Creation would not be there for us either and neither would the reality of Christ's gifts — the forgiveness of sins, life, and salvation. They would still be in our future.

Thus, the Formula of Agreement, by equating these two "practices" of Holy Communion, has as good as said, "It makes no difference whether Christ is "really, bodily" present in the bread and wine; one communion is as good as another." Let's see now: with Jesus or without Jesus — can they really be equated? The confessional insistence on Jesus' bodily presence in the sacrament is sacrificed for ecumenical conformity and the Lutheran Confessions and their constitutional subscription are violated again.

SACRIFICING THE GOSPEL

The full communion agreement with the Episcopal Church USA (ECUSA) not only sacrificed the confessional understanding of the "single order" of ministry but it sacrificed the preaching of the Gospel as well. "Called to Common Mission" (CCM) required the ELCA to set a human institution — the person of the bishop — as a "safeguard" for the gospel's authority.

Lutherans hold that the Word of God — the Gospel — is "self-authenticating," it needs no other authority added to it to make it genuine, authoritative, or effective. God "safeguards" his own Word. It only needs to be preached. Any of the baptized can do this. A public preacher — a pastor — needs only a "regular call." (See Appendix VII) "No," says ECUSA, "To be a pastor means having power and authority conferred upon him by the bishop in order to preach the gospel rightly and to deliver the presence of Christ in the Eucharist." Because it complied with that Episcopal demand, the ELCA no longer has a "self-authenticating" gospel. The bishop now "delegates" his authority to the person of the preacher in order to authenticate the gospel.

Through the adoption of CCM, the "historic episcopate" — a human rite — has been added to the Gospel. The ELCA no longer practices "Christ Alone" but Christ plus the bishop. As one pastor protested:

In accord with the Holy Scriptures and the Gospel of our Lord Jesus Christ, the Lutheran Confessions teach that Jesus Christ alone is the necessary cause of salvation, for "He alone is 'the Lamb of God, who takes away the sin of the world'" (Smalcald Articles, "Christ and Faith," Art. I, Par. 2). But CCM assails this teaching by requiring the adoption of the "historic episcopate" from the ECUSA, whose highest ecclesiastical court has ruled that the "historic episcopate" is a "core doctrine" ..."necessary for salvation, binding on all who are baptized" and "supplying a basis for reckoning a Church to be a true Church" (May, 15, 1996 bishops' ruling on the Chicago-Lambeth Quadrilateral). For this reason we stand in confessional protest against the implementation of CCM. CCM assails the sufficiency of Christ by requiring the acceptance of a human rite from the ECUSA which has been defined by the ECUSA as something "necessary for salvation." [38]

There's another reason why the office of bishop as established by the Historic Episcopate within ECUSA was and is objectionable. The practice was established by the "Act of Uniformity" — an order of the English Parliament in the 17th Century. This act was an instrument of religious intolerance. As a result of this "legislated uniformity," no pastor could preach in England unless said pastor had been ordained through the laying of hands by three bishops in the historic episcopate. One of the theologians opposing CCM has written:

By adopting CCM, the ELCA has pledged to conform its ordination structure and practice to the dictates of seventeenth-century, English episcopalian religious intolerance. The enforcement of this Act caused much persecution, suffering, and death. It is to be recalled that the Pilgrim Fathers (and mothers and children) came to the New World to escape this same religious intolerance and its violent consequences.

Although no one today would expect the Episcopal Church to enforce its episcopalianism against the ELCA with physically violent measures, episcopalian religious intolerance nevertheless is the driving force behind CCM. In order to achieve "full communion" with the Episcopal Church, the ELCA must incorporate the principles of this religious intolerance into its constitution and into the heart of its ordination structure and practice. Such conditions for unity could not be more contrary to the intentions of the Lutheran Reformers or to the aspirations of many who settled America.[39]

Through adoption of the historic Episcopate into the ELCA, the Ecumenized Agenda has taken the Gospel, the very Word of God which establishes the existence of the church itself and subjected it to the authority of a bishop and an instrument of religious intolerance.

SACRIFICING THE ARTICLE UPON WHICH THE CHURCH STANDS OR FALLS

In the Joint Declaration on the Doctrine of Justification (JDDJ)[40]--a 1999 agreement between Lutherans of the Lutheran World Federation and the Roman Catholic Church — the ELCA intended *"to show that on the basis of their dialogue the subscribing Lutheran churches and the Roman Catholic Church are now able to articulate a common understanding of our justification by God's grace through faith in Christ."*[41]

Martin Luther named this article declaring "justification by faith in Christ alone" as our "first and chief article."[42] Luther also declared "This is the article upon which the church stands or falls."[43] The ELCA, then, should take great care in how it treats this article. But it has not.

In its promotion of JDDJ the ELCA has agreed to the "demotion" — the sacrificing — of this article. In JDDJ "justification by faith alone" is no longer "**THE** article upon which the church stands or falls." It has been reduced from the "ONE" indispensible criterion to merely being ONE OF MANY criteria of supposedly equal importance.

Here's how one preacher put it: [Justification by faith alone] *is not merely "an indispensable criterion, which constantly serves to orient all the teaching and practice of our churches to Christ." (JDDJ, par 18) It is the indispensable criterion. When the Vatican succeeded in placing the indefinite article "an" before the words "indispensable criterion" within The Common Understanding of Justification it succeeded in displacing justification as the central article. An indispensable criterion cannot be the article on which the church stands or falls. It cannot be the central article. It can only be one indispensable criterion among several.*[44]

The truth of the above assessment is ratified when you realize that JDDJ was developed with the awareness that Pope John Paul II was still granting indulgences (indulgences were the "spark" that ignited the Reformation) at the time of JDDJ's supposed signing. The following is from an article in the New York Times:

"For Roman Catholics, the year 2000 offers early salvation.

Pope John Paul II announced today that in celebration of entering the third millennium of Christianity, penitents who do a charitable deed or give up cigarettes or alcohol for a day can earn an ''indulgence'' to eliminate punishment on earth or in purgatory. Church officials emphasize that indulgences depend on sincere repentance and are not a loophole for sinners. Still, some liberal Catholics are embarrassed by a practice that seems to offer a shortcut to salvation.

Indulgences are an ancient form of church-granted amnesty from certain forms of punishment, in this life or hereafter, for sin.

The medieval church sold indulgences, a practice that drove Martin Luther to rebel, beginning the Reformation. They remain a source of theological debate between Protestants and Catholics, and since Vatican II, the Roman Catholic Church had played down their importance.

By restoring indulgences to so prominent a position, John Paul II is making penitence a theme of the millennium celebration."[45]

In 1999, when it came time for the grand celebration of October 31ˢᵗ — the anniversary of Luther's nailing his 95 Theses to the chapel door at the university of Wittenberg, JDDJ was still so objectionable to some Lutherans and many Catholics that in order to have a ceremony at all, a different statement had to be put forward: the "Official Common Statement" (OCS). In the words of one historian:

The headline from an LWF news release dated 31 October 1999 reads, "Reformation Day in Augsburg was historic: Thousands witness signing of 'Joint Declaration' celebrations."

Unfortunately, in all its media releases, the LWF regularly fails to mention that the Joint Declaration was not signed in Augsburg, Germany. The OCS concludes with the seemingly innocuous phrase, "By this act of signing, The Catholic Church and The Lutheran World Federation confirm the Joint Declaration on the Doctrine of Justification in its entirety." In other words, the OCS was signed, not JDDJ.

So, you have to ask yourself, is the ELCA still committed to the exclusiveness of the article "justification by faith alone?" Or is presenting a "good work" in exchange for an "indulgence" its equal? JDDJ says they're the same thing. The Catholics couldn't agree to it; they would only confirm JDDJ's existence. In its willingness to give away its chief article for an empty celebration, the ELCA sacrificed its confession of the "article upon which the church stands or falls" to the altar of an Ecumenized Agenda.

SACRIFICING THE DIVINE

The ELCA has sacrificed 1) the biblical language for God, 2), the Word of God in its creative authority and 3) the biblical boundaries on sexual expression in order to achieve its Sexualized Agenda. Luther was well acquainted with the tactics employed here. These "sacrifices" are not original to the ELCA's church wide assembly actions. They weren't even original to Luther's circumstances when he authored his Catechisms in 1529. The three sacrifices carried out by the ELCA in its church wide expression originated in a garden. But Eden wasn't enough for its inhabitants: both man and woman sought god-like glory, violated Eden's boundaries, and exposed their sinful selves.

In writing the Catechisms of 1529, Luther used the Lord's Prayer to address the difference between theologians of the cross and theologians of glory. The first three petitions aptly address our current circumstances: Our Father who art in heaven:
- Hallowed be thy name;
- Thy kingdom come;
- Thy will be done

These petitions expose our sinful self, especially our capacity for idolatry:
- we want a god of our own choosing not the God who chooses us;
- we want a kingdom of our own establishment — visible and glorious — rather than God's kingdom hidden in faith and beneath the cross;
- we want to do what we want to do and call it "god's will" rather than actually suffering God's will to be done among us.

In these first petitions [of the Lord's Prayer] we are praying against ourselves and our pride; against the works of our hands and the rule of our human institutions; and against the willing of our own wills which are bound to will their own way. We are praying against the assertion: "God's work. Our hands." — the ELCA's heavily promoted tag line[46]

As we pray the rest of the Lord's Prayer petitions, strength, help and deliverance come when those who would distort the true God's Word are restrained; when the Holy Spirit works to keep us in faith, in Christ, and in the New Creation; and when God hinders and exposes the lies and deceptions of the devil, the world, and our sinful selves so that we can have peace and rest in the truth of God's Word.[47]

SACRIFICING THE BIBLICAL NAME FOR GOD

"Our Father who art in heaven, hallowed be Thy name…"   The decisions and actions of the ELCA's church wide expression give ample evidence of the sacrifice of the biblical name for God upon an altar of a Sexualized Agenda. They demonstrate that the supporters of those actions and decisions have wanted a god of their own choosing. They have rejected knowing the God who chooses them and gives them his name.

One only has to look at the official hymnal of the ELCA — Evangelical Lutheran Worship (the "cranberry" book). Masculine references to and masculine pronouns for God have been purged with a feminist fervor[48]. Not only have the psalms been so purged but many also have been rewritten from third person grammar into second person grammar with all the attendant alteration in meaning. Warrior and soldier language has mostly been excluded to the detriment of those honorable professions. The Triune Name of God: "Father, Son, and Holy Spirit," is made optional in the liturgies. It is now possible to worship in congregations of the ELCA and not hear the Triune Name of God for weeks and months on end.

As a further example of "disenfranchisement," none of the three expressions of the ELCA were given opportunity to "authorize" this new hymnal and its abandonment of the biblical name for God. The leadership produced this "resource." The CWA only had the opportunity to approve the "process" for producing it — not the "results" of the process. The content of the "new hymnal" was never up for a vote.

Talk about unaccountability! Perhaps they were concerned that someone would remind them of a greater accountability: "You shall not take the name of the Lord your God in vain."

SACRIFICING THE WORD OF GOD IN ITS CREATIVE AUTHORITY

"Our Father, who art in heaven… thy kingdom come" The decisions and actions of the ELCA's church wide expression in accomplishing a Sexualized Agenda give ample evidence of its sacrifice of the Word of God in its creative authority. The success of that agenda testifies to how powerfully we want a

kingdom of our own establishment — visible and glorious — rather than God's kingdom hidden in faith and beneath the cross.

God's Word is actively establishing two kingdoms: the one we know by sight and experience — this world — which is already passing away; and the one which we know (for now) only in promise and faith — the New Creation. It is already here in the person of Jesus Christ; but in Jesus Christ ALONE! Just as theologians of the cross must always be distinguishing Law and Gospel so too we always must be distinguishing justice and mercy, this world and the next. In desiring a kingdom of its own making, the ELCA has confused the kingdoms and abandoned what is necessary to distinguish them. Here's how I've put it previously:

> *Through the multitude of vocations God gives his creatures, we're put to work. God charges us, as instruments of his left and right hand rule, to love his creation. Seeing that everyone gets what they deserve and deserves what they get is our task of justice. Yet justice cannot rule alone for, left to itself, the rule of justice drives to tyranny. So, mercy must rule as well; but it, too, cannot rule alone. Alone, the rule of mercy lapses into anarchy. Here, then, is yet another paradox to hold in tension: justice and mercy. In that difficult — impossible-for-creatures-to-maintain — paradoxical tension between justice and mercy, we come to know the trials of love. Careening between the poles of tyranny and anarchy, we creatures can only trust in the creation-sustaining-redeeming work of our Creator God who is love itself.*[49]

So by legislative action, the ELCA 2009 CWA determined that the mercy of God is a "general" principle. It can be established by the political process. They put their hands to work in the casting of ballots. They made a legislative decision and — in their presumption to glory — declared that by their enacting of such a "law," they were accomplishing God's work of mercy. They assumed for themselves the work of knowing good and evil, usurping the Word's creative authority to address sinners and "clarify" them — so that those sinners would know the truth about themselves and God.

As you will learn in the next sub-section, God has set definite boundaries around sexual behavior and the expression of our sexual desires. I have been careful throughout this treatise to refrain from naming people who engage in same-sex behavior as "homosexuals." To do so would be to "aid and abet" their self-naming which denies God's Word in its creative authority — the authority with which he named them "male and female."

There is no other human identity than a heterosexual identity! (See Appendix XI) In this creation broken by sin people have "preferences" for what excites them sexually. Just because they may prefer sexual expression with others of the same sex, they have no "justification" to call themselves "homosexual." The bible knows of no "homosexuals" only heterosexuals who — in their behavior — express their sexual desires with others of the same sex. Now in this generation — these sinners want to name themselves, saying that God — in his word, the bible — doesn't know them. Oh, really? The issue is about BEHAVIOR! It's not about an "orientation" or a "nature."

Speaking historically, there have always been members of the church who have engaged in homosexual behavior AND in every generation of the church there have been pastors and priests who engaged in it and other "out-of-bounds" sexual behavior.

The church has dealt with these "out-of-bounds" sexual behaviors as a matter of confession and forgiveness; that is, its preachers brought the Word of God face-to-face with the sinner and delivered it "for you." The living, active Word of God as the two-edged sword of Law and Gospel was spoken to the sinner in all its external and internal clarity. In such delivery there is NO AMBIGUITY: Jesus Christ is handed over so that by the grace of God sinners will be put to a merciful death and saints raised up to walk in newness of life.[50] The person of the preacher delivered the person of Jesus Christ to the person of the sinner so that the Word of God in all its creative authority could "create" a forgiven saint where once there had only been a condemned sinner. You can't get much more particular and personal than that!

When the person's persistent "out-of-bounds" behavior demonstrated that the church could no longer trust the person, legal or coercive remedies were employed. Now, I admit that some in the church have been quick in their rush to judgment and that coercive — even violent — remedies have been excessive at times. However, the occasional coercive "remedy" can't be used as an excuse to legislatively deny the creative power of God's Word in the personal and particular application of the pronoun "for you!" Such "quick rush to judgment, though," does expose the serious and disruptive consequences of sexual behavior when it gets outside the boundaries set for it by the external clarity of God's Word; that is, God's first use of the Law.

In this generation some people practicing homosexual behavior have felt the restraining effects of God's accusation as he's used the Law upon them. Rebelling against that restraint, they hide from knowing the truth about themselves and God. They refuse to hear God's Word in its personal and particular address. They refuse because the "for you" is God's living, active Word and it is a two-edged sword — judging, condemning, and driving down to death. And death is a fearsome thing, but there... and there only is where the Word gives life.

So, because some people practicing homosexual behavior refuse to be dealt with in the particular and in person by God's Word, they have convinced the ELCA's CWA to deal with them in general through a human word.

The law, sin and repentance get short shrift, becoming more and more airy and abstract. The gospel loses its christocentric specificity, becoming an ideology of universal acceptance. As H. Richard Niebuhr put it in a classic line from another generation, "a God without wrath brings men without sin into a kingdom without pain through the ministrations of a Christ without a cross." [51]

They have sacrificed God's Word in its creative authority for the advancement of a Sexualized Agenda.

SACRIFICING THE BIBLICAL BOUNDARIES ON SEXUAL EXPRESSION

"Our Father, who art in heaven... thy will be done" Biblical boundaries regarding sexual behavior and expression have been sacrificed by the success of the Sexualized Agenda. Proving themselves sinners, the advocates of that agenda demonstrate just how desperately we — of a fallen humanity — crave doing what we want to do and call it "god's" will rather than actually suffering God's will to be done among us.

The social statement and the resolutions accomplish this kind of idolatry because they've replaced the Word of God in its "external clarity" with an interpretation from their own minds. The Bible, the Holy Scriptures as the Word of God, clearly sets forth the boundaries around sexual behavior. The only reason for "ambiguity" is because sinners don't like what they hear. Mark Twain was known to comment: *"It's not what I don't understand in the Bible that troubles me; it's what I do understand."*

These boundaries are like a "hedge of protection." (Job 1:10) They protect what's inside from what's outside. You who have built and maintained fences for the protection of livestock — anyone who has built and maintained fences for the protection of property and the preservation of privacy — you know the importance of fences to protect what's inside of them and the importance of clear and well-established boundaries to neighborly relationships. But... compare these words of the poet Robert Frost: *"Something there is that doesn't love a wall."* (See Appendix XV)

The Word of God in its creative authority has given humanity the "gift" of sexual expression AND set forth out a "hedge of protection" around the "garden" in which humanity is to enjoy that gift. In a myriad of ways the stories of the bible's people give testimony to the destructive power of sexual expression when the fences are broken, when the "hedge of protection is torn down," when the boundaries are violated. Certainly, our cultural experience of recent decades bears witness as well to the pervasive power of sexual expression when it is loosed from its boundaries; it takes over: everything is "sexualized." Certainly, our personal experience may give testimony, too — albeit confidential — to the devastating consequences of sexual expression unchecked by its biblical fences.

The Word of God in its creative authority has established this "garden" for the enjoyment of human sexuality:

"Then the man said, "This at last is bone of my bones and flesh of my flesh; she shall be called Woman, because she was taken out of Man." Therefore a man shall leave his father and his mother and hold fast to his wife, and they shall become one flesh." (Genesis 2:23-24)

And again the Word of God declares:

[Jesus said] "Have you not read that he who created them from the beginning made them male and female, and said, 'Therefore a man shall leave his father and his mother and hold fast to his wife, and the two shall become one flesh'? So they are no longer two but one flesh. What therefore God has joined together let not man separate." (Matthew 19:4-6)

Through its creative authority the Word of God "speaks" into being a garden for the enjoyment of sexual expression and begins building the hedge of protection around it. That protection increases in strength as other forms of sexual expression are declared "out-of-bounds." Those forms include:

- Homosexual behavior (sexual intercourse between persons of the same sex),[52]

- Fornication (sexual intercourse between unmarried persons)[53],
- Adultery (sexual intercourse with someone who is not your marriage partner)[54],
- Incest (sexual intercourse with close family) [55],
- Pedophilia (sexual intercourse with children)[56],
- Bestiality (sexual intercourse with animals) [57],
- Prostitution (sexual intercourse for money)[58],
- Onanism (interrupting sexual intercourse so as to avoid pregnancy)[59], and
- Divorce (sexual intercourse by serial adultery)[60]

In order to further protect the garden of marriage--that is, sexual intercourse between a man and a woman within a monogamous, faithful marriage established by vows before witnesses[61] — in order to protect that garden, the Word of God delivers harsh labels and consequences upon sexual behavior which violates the sanctity of the garden. Harsh labels such as "sin," "curse," and "abomination" control sexual behavior by the power of shame. [62] Harsh consequences — up to and including the death penalty (by disease or legal means) — control sexual behavior through the fear of consequences. These labels and consequences are God employing the Law in its First Use to maintain order, to keep the boundaries, to establish the "hedged in garden." It matters not how many poets plead *"Something there is that doesn't love a wall."* (See Appendix XV) God will "order" sinners, even order them to death — just so he can raise them to new life!

Now — bearing the above in mind — and contrary to the "talking points" used to promote and defend the assembly's affirmative vote, this issue is NOT about welcoming "gays" into the church nor is it about hospitality nor is it about salvation or excluding homosexuals from "heaven." Those "talking point" issues are raised as "diversions" meant to direct our attention away from the real issue: the sacrifice of the biblical boundaries upon the altar of a Sexualized Agenda.

CONCLUSION

All this "human" advancing of the Politicized, Ecumenized, and Sexualized Agendas has resulted in numerous instances of sacrifice. By decision after decision the institutional ELCA, the actions of the CWA, and their supporters have put the Lutheran Confessions and God's Word on a human altar and sacrificed them to a set of human agendas. This human work has taken the ELCA down the path of heresy, through schism, and into apostasy. That work has "unchurched" me and those who recall with loyalty the strength and uniqueness of our Lutheran tradition and the necessity of "Christ Alone!"

THE PATH

TO

CONFESSING:

GOD TALK

Therefore, I say
- to the voting members of the ELCA's 2009 CWA who voted in the affirmative for the "sexual" issues;
- to the ELCA's institutional leadership who have through the years promoted agendas which have resulted in the ELCA's heterodoxy, unchurching, confusion, and apostasy;
- to the members of the ELCA — pastors and lay — who celebrate these decisions and their results

YOU ARE WRONG! REPENT AND BELIEVE!
YOUR SINS ARE FORGIVEN FOR JESUS' SAKE.
IN THE NAME OF THE FATHER, AND OF THE SON+
AND OF THE HOLY SPIRIT. AMEN

SILENCE IS **NOT** AN OPTION!

Even when confronted by an ecclesial juggernaut of unaccountable authority like the ELCA's church wide expression, we cannot be intimidated into silence: "Even the stones will cry out!" (Luke 19:40) God is busy even now raising up "wild" prophets from among the people. He is calling them out of the hinter land. He has sent out his Word like a hammer to break stony hearts so that they will cry out with Good News. We are bound to stand and confess:

- For the sake of the Gospel
- For the sake of the next generation
- For the sake of those who would be our fellow confessors
- For the sake of the truth.

We must stand and confess for the sake of the Gospel. Some of us have ordination vows to tend. All of us have our baptismal prerogative to exercise. Together let us preach the gospel in all its purity and deliver the sacraments according to that gospel so that we and those who assemble with us will enjoy the one holy Christian church. Together let us stand and confess God's living and active Word as the two-edged sword of Law and Gospel so that the false and apostate church will be exposed for what it is—an imposter.

We must stand and confess for the sake of the next generation. The apostolic faith of Jesus Christ as the Way, the Truth, and the Life must be delivered to them. For their sake we must confess the Word of God to them in all its creative authority, preaching to them in such a way that they receive the "real and bodily" presence of Jesus Christ handed over particularly "for you!" For the sake of their enjoying Christ's benefits of the forgiveness of sins, life, and salvation, we must distinguish for them the "false gospel" of tolerance, acceptance, and inclusivity.[63]

We must stand and confess for the sake of those who would be our fellow confessors. God is right now raising them up, calling them forth just like he's calling you forth. Together, you will be one another's preachers so that you don't have to "look within" but can trust the gospel that is being preached to you, one to the other. Together, let us bear witness—to one another and to those whose hearts are still hardened—that God's Word, though it be a hammer upon stones, is the creative authority which beats hard-hearted sinners to death in order to raise them up to new life in Christ.

We must stand and confess for the sake of the Truth. You learned from me at the outset (page 8) that there was a larger dimension to this struggle. We are at a cross-road in history. The powerful have always claimed their right to ask "What is the truth?" and then define it in a way most beneficial for them. That has not changed. Their "truth" has always been "falsifiable" by a check with reality. Especially when the reality that there is THE Truth which will not deal with them on the basis of power but only in the truth, exposes them for the sinners they are.

But now in this generation the powerful are claiming "There is NO truth!" There are only agendas. The agendas of each individual self, looking within in order find its own interpretation, meaning, and conclusion. The "self" and its desires set the agenda.

We are called to stand and confess in these times when world views and philosophical systems contend for control — not just over which truth will be true — but for the right of any truth to exist at all.

For simplicity's sake I'll label those who stand for the existence of truth to be Modernity; and I'll label those who would deny the existence of any truth to be Post-Modernity. For Modernity — though it contends over the truth — there is still truth. Within that truth one can still declare that there is an ultimate Truth, and one can still preach that that ultimate Truth is none other than Jesus Christ. For Post-Modernity, there is no truth, only power — the power to manipulate the symbols of culture for the success of various agendas.

Take words for example. They're symbols in a culture's language. In Modernity's philosophical world-view words are symbols that are attached to a reality. Sometimes that reality is substantial, tangible and physical — like table, rock, or elephant. Sometimes that reality is ephemeral, intangible, and non-physical — like an idea, concept, or emotion. Whatever sort of reality to which words as symbols may be attached, the words convey that reality to their reader or hearer. In this sense you could say that this is a "charismatic" use of words; that is, they convey the speaker's reality to the hearer in such a way that it becomes "invested" in the hearer.

For Post-Modernity's philosophical world-view, words are symbols unattached to reality. They have no necessary connection to anything tangible or intangible. They just are. When a Post-Modern speaks, he intends that you will invest his words with whatever meaning you want them to have. In this sense you could say that this is a "glamorous" use of words. They don't convey the speaker's reality to you. There is no reality to convey. The words are just symbols waiting for the hearer to fill them with meaning.

This difference has serious consequences for the truth. Because the Modern speaker's words still bear a connection — an attachment — to reality, his hearers still have the means to distinguish true from false: they can check out the reality and see how it compares with the speaker's words. If they can't check out the reality, they can at least recall their own reality and their past experience in similar situations, distinguishing true from false in that manner. Likewise, they can also compare the Modern's speaker's words to other truths — maybe even the ultimate Truth — as a way of distinguishing true from false. The speaker remains constrained by the existence of reality and its truth.

But a Post-Modern speaker is not so constrained. His words are symbols awaiting fulfillment from the reality of his hearers. For him there are no constraints imposed by his own reality. His words were never meant to convey his reality but to invite his hearers to give it their own. In this manner a Post-Modern speaker's words will mean one thing to one person and mean something else to another person. The words convey no meaning — just the opportunity to be given meaning by the hearer for the satisfaction of some post-modern agenda.

The difference between Modernity and Post-Modernity has even greater consequences for our culture's knowledge of God. Either the word "God" is a symbol connected to an actual underlying reality of which one can say things are either true or false; or, the word "God" is a symbol unconnected to any reality and is just an empty word waiting to be "filled" with meaning by those who hear it.

This conflict of world views, and philosophical systems has an outcome which holds the potential to rob our culture of any sense of order, predictability, or truth. If Post-Modernity prevails, power, not truth, will order our culture. Since there will be no truth, whatever person, group, or ideology wielding the power will be able to establish their agenda — the collective desires of their sinful selves — with no accountability and no curb on their authority. They will have achieved — at least for this world — what the tempter promised in the garden — "you shall be like gods…"

We must stand and confess

- for the sake of the gospel of Jesus Christ
- for the sake of the generation to come;
- for the sake of our fellow confessors; and
- for the survival of the truth itself.

WHAT THEN SHALL WE SAY (OR DO)?

Be resolute!

You are NOT being divisive by standing and confessing.

You are not the "trouble makers" if you stand and confess:

- You are confessing that the church is the assembly of believers among whom the gospel is rightly preached and the sacraments rightly given.
- You are confessing that the church is NOT an assembly of people gathered around a false gospel of tolerance, acceptance, and inclusivity.
- You are confessing that the ELCA has taken the path through heresy, by schism, into apostasy and it no longer preaches the gospel purely.

--Be resolute! Jesus said, *"In this world you will have troubles; but take heart, I have overcome the world."* (John 16:33)

Become a Confessor:

It is my hope you will become a confessor as I have. If so, then sign up!

If you have questions that need answering before you can become a confessor, please ask.

If you remain unconvinced and have no conviction which to confess, then I will declare the gospel of Jesus Christ to you: Your sins are forgiven for Jesus sake! Amen

If your heart is hardened in opposition, then you are wrong! Repent and believe! Your sins are forgiven for Jesus' sake! In the name of the Father, and of the Son, and of the Holy Spirit. Amen

Become a "fellow" Confessor:

It is my hope that if you subscribe to this confession, you will promote it in your home, your congregation, and your community. Share it with your friends and family.

It is my hope that confessors and congregations, groups of confessors and groups of congregations will stand and confess together.

Become a Confessing Church Council and Congregation

I sincerely desire that church councils would take a stand together and confess the pure gospel of Jesus Christ, joining me "in statu confessionis." But, you — as church councils — can take NO LEGISLATIVE ACTION to coerce confession. The only authority we have as Christians is to preach a sermon.

This I have done through this treatise. I will declare to you the living, active Word of God whose creative power comes upon us as the two-edged sword of Law and Gospel. *"The kingdom of God is at hand! Repent and Believe!"* If that Word is not sufficient, then no vote — however large the majority — should coerce agreement in the law where there is none in the gospel.

If, however, there is unanimity of confessing, then take this confession before the congregation. See to it that they receive this preaching as well. Again, do not coerce uniformity. But if all confess, then together as a congregation we will declare *"in statu confessionis."*

Whatever number of council members and congregation members do confess, I will welcome your company. To those who do not confess, the Lord is not done with you.

Taking action without the unanimous confession of council
Confessing is the work of the gospel for the sake of the gospel. Here are other actions which can be accomplished through legislative decisions — the appropriate "ordering" function of the Law.

--You can vote to adopt "protective" legislation in your constitution and by-laws (See Appendix XVIII)

--You can vote to affiliate with a protest or renewal group: Word Alone and Lutheran Core are nation-wide organizations. (See Appendix XVI)

--You can vote to send a resolution to the Synod Council or Synod Assembly registering your protest and requesting redress. (See Appendix I)

--You can find other congregations and vote to affiliate with them in a local or synodical protest group.

--You can vote to redirect your congregation's benevolence so that you are not "feeding" the unaccountable authority that is the ELCA.

--You can form chapters or missions of alternative Lutheran bodies in anticipation of a negative outcome to our *"in statu confessionis."* The ELCA has no constitutional prohibition against "dual" membership. (see Appendix XVII)

--You can begin the process of leaving the ELCA. The purpose of *"in statu confessionis"* is to avoid having to do this. But, if the ELCA does not "repent" at its church wide assembly in 2011, our *"in statu confessionis"* will have come to an end and it will be time to leave.

REMEMBER: the time for talking is ended. The time for confessing is at hand! Distribute this book, invite confession, answer questions, but DO NOT ARGUE with the hard-hearted. The only answer to the absolute refusal of "hardened hearts" is to declare the Absolution: forgive them their sins!

APPENDICES

APPENDIX I -- A RESOLUTION IN OPPOSITION TO THE ACTIONS OF THE 2009 CHURCHWIDE ASSEMBLY

WHEREAS, the 2009 Churchwide Assembly of the ELCA has adopted the social statement, "Human Sexuality: Gift and Trust", and

WHEREAS, in Part IV (lines 620 – 628 in the Pre-Assembly Report) this statement reads:
The historic Christian tradition and the Lutheran Confessions have recognized marriage as a covenant between a man and a woman, reflecting Mark 10: 6–9: "But from the beginning of creation, God made them male and female. For this reason a man shall leave his father and mother and be joined to his wife, and the two shall become one flesh. So they are no longer two, but one flesh. Therefore what God has joined together, let no one put asunder." (Jesus here recalls Genesis 1:27; 2:23–24.), and

WHEREAS, in Part IV (lines 740 – 744, as amended, of the Pre-Assembly Report) it reads:
Recognizing that this conclusion differs from the historic Christian tradition and the Lutheran Confessions, some people, though not all, in this church and within the larger Christian community, conclude that marriage is also the appropriate term to use in describing similar benefits, protection, and support for same-gender couples entering into lifelong monogamous relationships, and

WHEREAS, the statement then goes on to treat these two positions and the variants within them as of equal validity, on the basis of the "conscience-bound beliefs" of those who hold them (Part IV, lines 809 – 868 of the Pre-Assembly Report), and

WHEREAS, on this same basis of the "conscience-bound lack of consensus in this church" (lines 452 – 453 of the Report and Recommendation on Ministry Policies in Part V of the Pre-Assembly Report) the resolutions on ministry policies (SA09.05.23 – 24 – 26 & 27) were adopted, and

WHEREAS, neither the Social Statement nor the Recommendation on Ministry Policies present an argument based on Scripture, the Lutheran Confessions and with the aid of sound reason either to reject what is admitted to be the position of the historic Christian tradition and the Lutheran Confessions based on Scripture or to accept a position which is admitted to be contrary to the historic Christian tradition and the Lutheran Confessions, and

WHEREAS, the Confession of Faith of the ELCA (Chapter 2 of the ELCA Constitution) commits the ELCA to accept the canonical Scriptures as the authoritative source and norm of our proclamation, faith and life, and to accept the confessional writings of the Lutheran Church as a true witness of the Gospel and valid interpretations of the faith of the Church, therefore, be it

RESOLVED, that the Northeastern Iowa Synod Council, repudiate the decisions of the 2009 Churchwide Assembly in adopting the social statement "Human Sexuality: Gift and Trust" and the 4 Resolutions on Ministry Policies (CA09.05.23 – 24 – 26 & 27) as violations of the Confession of Faith, Chapter 2 of the ELCA Constitution, and be it further

RESOLVED, that the Northeastern Iowa Synod Council memorialize the ELCA Church Council to repudiate these actions as violations of the Confession of Faith, Chapter 2 of the ELCA Constitution, refuse to implement these actions, and begin the process to overturn these decisions at the 2011 Churchwide Assembly

APPENDIX II – ELCA Constitutional Confession of Faith

Chapter 2.
CONFESSION OF FAITH
2.01. This church confesses the Triune God, Father, Son, and Holy Spirit.

2.02. This church confesses Jesus Christ as Lord and Savior and the Gospel as the power of God for the salvation of all who believe.

- Jesus Christ is the Word of God incarnate, through whom everything was made and through whose life, death, and resurrection God fashions a new creation.
- The proclamation of God's message to us as both Law and Gospel is the Word of God, revealing judgment and mercy through word and deed, beginning with the Word in creation, continuing in the history of Israel, and centering in all its fullness in the person and work of Jesus Christ.
- The canonical Scriptures of the Old and New Testaments are the written Word of God. Inspired by God's Spirit speaking through their authors, they record and announce God's revelation centering in Jesus Christ. Through them God's Spirit speaks to us to create and sustain Christian faith and fellowship for service in the world.

2.03. This church accepts the canonical Scriptures of the Old and New Testaments as the inspired Word of God and the authoritative source and norm of its proclamation, faith, and life.

2.04. This church accepts the Apostles', Nicene, and Athanasian Creeds as true declarations of the faith of this church.

2.05. This church accepts the Unaltered Augsburg Confession as a true witness to the Gospel, acknowledging as one with it in faith and doctrine all churches that likewise accept the teachings of the Unaltered Augsburg Confession.

2.06. This church accepts the other confessional writings in the Book of Concord, namely, the Apology of the Augsburg Confession, the Smalcald Articles and the Treatise, the Small Catechism, the Large Catechism, and the Formula of Concord, as further valid interpretations of the faith of the Church.

2.07. This church confesses the Gospel, recorded in the Holy Scripture and confessed in the ecumenical creeds and Lutheran confessional writings, as the power of God to create and sustain the Church for God's mission in the world.[64]

APPENDIX III

Ordination Vows in the ELCA

The presiding minister questions the ordinand/s.
Before almighty God, to whom you must give account,
and in the presence of this assembly, I ask:

Will you assume this office, believing that the church's call is God's call to the ministry of word and sacrament?
Each ordinand responds: I will, and I ask God to help me.

The church in which you are to be ordained confesses that the Holy Scriptures are the word of God and are the norm of its faith and life. We accept, teach, and confess the Apostles', the Nicene, and the Athanasian Creeds. We also acknowledge the Lutheran Confessions as true witnesses and faithful expositions of the Holy Scriptures. Will you therefore preach and teach in accordance with the Holy Scriptures and these creeds and confessions?
Each ordinand responds: I will, and I ask God to help me.

Will you be diligent in your study of the Holy Scriptures and faithful in your use of the means of grace? Will you pray for God's people, nourish them with the word and sacraments,
and lead them by your own example in faithful service and holy living?
Each ordinand responds: I will, and I ask God to help me.

Will you give faithful witness in the world, that God's love may be known in all that you do?
Each ordinand responds: I will, and I ask God to help me.

Almighty God, who has given you the will to do these things,
graciously give you the strength and compassion to perform them.
The assembly responds: **Amen.**[65]

APPENDIX IV -- The Necessity of Resistance

Approved April 27, 2009 by the WordAlone Network Annual Convention and referred to Lutheran CORE for consideration.

First, the biblical witness concerning marriage, the family and sexual practices has established an historic consensus which has held ecumenically throughout the church's history. This long term and virtually universal consensus of interpretation demonstrates compellingly that the biblical word has functioned clearly and authoritatively on the issues. Whatever ambiguities remain have been and can be clarified in light of this agreement. Those who wish to change the accepted guidelines and expectations for clergy in the ELCA have yet to justify the reconsideration of issues settled by the Scripture and accepted by all but a minuscule minority of Christians.

Secondly, while appealing for unity, the proposal presented for the decision of the Minneapolis churchwide assembly is in fact profoundly divisive. All of the evidence available demonstrates that Roman Catholics, the Orthodox, and most Protestants strongly oppose changing the biblical standards. Voting for the proposed changes will thus take the Evangelical Lutheran Church in America out of the stated biblical and ecumenical consensus of the church, isolating it from the visible unity with other Christians.

Thirdly, the proposal presented for action by the church council of the ELCA at its Minneapolis churchwide assembly in August of 2009 brings the church into a state of confession — as defined by Article X of the Formula of Concord — in two ways. It proposes to compromise the plain sense of Scripture, setting aside the authority of the biblical word. Further, if the ecumenical consensus is overturned by vote of the churchwide assembly, the majority would forcibly remove those who oppose such changes from the historic and virtually universal consensus prevailing in the one, holy, catholic and apostolic church. As such, the proposal presented by the church council is both schismatic and coercive.

Declaring this proposal in statu confessionis, that is, declaring a state of confession means that the proposed action must be resisted on biblical grounds. This opposition takes the form of refusing to support those institutions and officers of the ELCA who have betrayed their true purposes. It is incumbent on the officers of the church, its bishops and pastors, all of whom have taken oaths to preach and teach according to the Scripture and the Lutheran Confession to join this resistance. Their failure to respect their promises has placed the Evangelical Lutheran Church in America in schism.[66]

Appendix V

Lutheran Confessional Writings[67]

The Augsburg Confession:
Article Seven — The Office of the Ministry

To obtain such faith God instituted the office of the ministry; that is, provided the Gospel and the sacraments. Through these, as through means, he gives the Holy Spirit, who works faith, when and where he pleases, in those who hear the Gospel. And the Gospel teaches that we have a gracious God, not by our own merits but by the merit of Christ, when we believe this.

Condemned are the Anabaptists and others who teach that the Holy Spirit comes to us through our own preparations, thoughts, and works without the external word of the Gospel.

The Augsburg Confession:
Article Seven — The Church

It is also taught among us that one holy Christian church will be and remain forever. This is the assembly of all believers among whom the Gospel is preached in its purity and the holy sacraments are administered according to the Gospel. For it is sufficient for the true unity of the Christian church that the Gospel be preached in conformity with a pure understanding of it and that the sacraments be administered in accordance with the divine Word. It is not necessary for the true unity of the Christian church that ceremonies, instituted by men, should be observed uniformly in all places. It is as Paul says in Eph. 4:4, 5 "There is one body and one Spirit just as you were called to the one hope that belongs to your call, one Lord, one faith, one baptism."

The Augsburg Confession:
Article XIV Order in the Church

It is taught among us that nobody should publically teach or preach or administer the sacraments in the church without a regular call.

Appendix VI
Lutheran Clergy:
Luther and the Reformers so re-visioned the clergy that you could say the clergy--as an ontological category distinct from the laity--ceased to exist. They denied the clergy as a person ontologically changed into a repository of grace. Which grace could then be dispensed in varying amounts by priest, bishop, or pope. They announced all the baptized are priests. All the baptized have been graced by the revelation of their life in two kingdoms. All have the calling to announce and bear witness to this revelatory existence so that all people would have faith and be made disciples. This calling is the office or ministry of Word and Sacrament, which is given that all may have faith.

The pastoral office of public ministry is different from the office or ministry of Word and Sacrament. The latter is given to all the baptized, the priesthood of all believers. This is convincingly attested to in the Augustana which describes the common life of all Christians for thirteen articles before it deals with the "public" ministry. The process of "rightly" calling (ordering) someone to bear the responsibility of publicly preaching and teaching is a legal matter within the institution--no more or less spiritual than any other selection process. Certainly, there is recognition of certain gifts within the one being called, but those gifts are vocational gifts. Every other vocation which is given for the building up of the body receives vocational gifts from the Holy Spirit as well.

Clergy, then, are a phenomenological category, not an ontological one. Only under the experience of being called by a congregation (or some other external means) and engaged in public preaching through verbal or visible proclamation or in the act of teaching is one a "clergy." Clergy or pastor becomes a vocational title in the same way that you would label someone a plumber or a doctor. There can be no ontological claim to the title. When one is not under call and no longer publicly preaching and teaching, that one is not clergy or pastor. Most of the duties that have gathered by accretion to the pastoral office, such as prayer, visiting the sick, etc., are those which are common to all Christians. Making those duties part of the pastoral office has become detrimental to the common Christian life as Christians have assumed the pastor does it in their stead.

With clergy being phenomenologically defined there is nothing except the Word and its use to identify the church. One cannot point to a person and say, "There is the church." Neither can one say that a certain kind of person, i.e. an ontologically changed clergy, is necessary for the church. All that is needed is a voice and any of the baptized (who in that baptism have been ordained to preach the gospel) can provide that voice for in them has been revealed the only ontology necessary--the 200% life in two kingdoms.[68]

--the Reverend Timothy J. Swenson

Appendix VII

Fragments from "The Vision of the ELCA"

Lutherans may differ in evaluating the difference between the sixteenth century and the present. Some Lutherans in the Evangelical Lutheran Church in America hold that unity was already broken when the confessors presented the Augsburg Confession in 1530; others hold that the confessors were attempting to maintain a unity that still existed. But all agree that the "satis est" of Augsburg Confession VII established an ecumenical principle as valid today as it was in 1530. Augsburg Confession VII continues to be ecumenically liberating because of its claim that the truth of the Gospel is the catholic faith and is sufficient for the true unity of the church.

In today's denominationalism the satis est provides an ecumenical resource and basis to move to growing levels of fellowship [i.e., communion] among divided churches. Article VII remains fundamental for Lutheran ecumenical activity; its primary meaning is that only those things that convey salvation, justification by grace through faith, are allowed to be signs and constitutive elements of the church. Yet, for all its cohesiveness and precision, Article VII does not present a complete doctrine of the church. It is not in the first instance an expression of a falsely understood ecumenical openness and freedom from church order, customs, and usages in the church. What it says is essential for understanding the unity of the church, but does not exhaust what must be said. The primary meaning of Article VII is that only those things that convey salvation, justification by grace through faith, are allowed to be signs and constitutive elements of the church. It is also necessary to recognize the evangelical and ecclesiological implications of the missionary situation of the global church in our time, which did not exist in the 16th century.

Article VII of the Augsburg Confession continues to be ecumenically freeing because of its insistence that agreement in the Gospel suffices for Christian unity. As Lutherans seek to enter into fellowship without insisting on doctrinal or ecclesiastical uniformity, they place an ecumenical emphasis on common formulation and expression of theological consensus on the Gospel. There is room for recognizing, living and experiencing fellowship within the context of seeking together larger theological agreement, of constantly searching critically for the theological truth of the Gospel to be proclaimed together in the present critical time of our world.

Appendix VIII

The Historic Episcopate by *J. Robert Wright, an Episcopalian and one of the authors of the Concordat,*

Definition
Let me offer a definition of the historic episcopate, which I think will resonate with what the Episcopal Church believes, although I am sure that Lutherans who understand it will, and should, explain it in their own ways. (After all, there are probably as many different definitions of the historic episcopate among Episcopalians as I have encountered definitions of justification among Lutherans!)

The historic episcopate is a succession of bishops or church leaders whose roots are planted in the time of the early church, pointing back to the centrality of Christ and the teaching of the apostles, pointing to the biblical canon, the creeds, and the councils, while at the same time pointing forward in order to oversee, or superintend, or give leadership to, the mission of the church today.

In the words of the 1982 Lima statement on *Baptism, Eucharist, and Ministry* from the Faith and Order Commission of the World Council of Churches, representative of widespread international agreement and whose director at that time was an American Lutheran, the historic episcopate is "a sign though not a guarantee," in personal terms, of the unity and continuity of the church's faith throughout time and space.

It points towards a unity of the church, a communion of churches, that is greater than any one denomination or local judicature, at the same time that it points toward the spiritual, missiological, and doctrinal continuity of the church of today with the church of the ages. It is still accepted and practiced by some three-fourths of the world's Christians and is the only ministerial institution that exists to promote the unity and mutual responsibility of the worldwide church.

The Episcopal Church believes that this sign — this teaching about the historic episcopate — which has ancient roots and finds global expression, is (in the words of our 1982 General Convention, which I shall unpack in a few moments) "essential to the reunion of the church" even though we do not believe it is necessary to salvation nor a condition for recognizing the churchly character of other churches.

It is the sign conveyed by installing or ordaining a new bishop by prayer for the gift of the Holy Spirit with the laying on of hands by at least three other bishops already sharing in the historic episcopate as testimony that something more than local interest is involved in the ministry of oversight within the church.[69]

Appendix IX

The Authority of the Gospel

The church's earliest creed, Jesus Christ is Lord, asserts an ultimate claim regarding the risen Christ that at the same time renders every other form of authority secondary. This is already apparent in the New Testament itself, which repeatedly returns to the theme. "All authority in heaven and on earth has been given to me," Christ says as he sends his disciples into mission (Matt. 28:19). His overall sovereignty is the hope of all creation: "...at his cominq, every knee shall bow, on the earth, above the earth and under the earth..." (Phil. 2:i0}. At the same time, it makes every other institution and power provisional: "then comes the end, when he hands over the kingdom to God the Father, after he has destroyed every ruler and very authority and power," (1 Cor. 15:24).

In the Lutheran Confessions, Christ's ultimacy is set out in two dimensions: in the authority of the word and in the critique generated over and against offices, which seek to claim it for themselves. The priority of the word again grows out of New Testament roots. "He who hears you hears me," Jesus says in his sending (Luke 10:16). The crucified and risen Lord continues his work in and through the spoken word, whether in its preached or sacramental form. As such, God's word--the word that creates and became incarnate — has become a human word, fit for the lips of his sinners.

It is critical to note that precisely in its incarnate form, where it might be taken as one opinion among countless others, the word retains the power of its ultimate speaker. Christ is the word. As Article V of the Augustana states, by his Spirit, the preached and sacramental word carries out his purpose, affecting faith in the hearer.

The contrast between the gospel and other forms of speech can be seen in relation to the law: "The law says do this, and it is never done. The gospel says, 'Believe in this,' and it is done already," Luther argues in the Heidelberg Disputations. The law can only signify, pointing away from itself to an action required or under interdict. Its target is the will of the hearer, which is assumed to provide the power necessary to compliance. The gospel is performative — precisely in, with and under all the other human words, it does what it says, carrying the hearer beyond alternatives as it actually creates faith, bestows freedom, engenders joy, finally raises the dead. Such claims can be made for the gospel because of the Spirit who animates it.[70]

--James Arne Nestingen

APPENDIX X

Fragments from: "A Biblical Approach to Human Sexuality" by Merton Strommen

Our struggle with human sexuality is as old as the "fall" in the Garden of Eden and will be with us until time ends. Even with "our" best attempts to control it we often fall; and once we stop seeking God's help we're hopelessly outmatched by the enemy and his evil plans for us. We have, in the last 40 years, steadily yielded to the idea that our sexual urges are uncontrollable, and now we are living with the consequences of that decision. A decision which has resulted in the pain and brokenness around us and from which we have no fruit to show for all our "progress and scientific enlightenment". Rampant sexual abuse, teenage sex and pregnancies, infidelity, spreading sexual diseases and a growing disrespect for human life are all evidence of the growing lack of control of our sexuality as God intended it....

...What, therefore, should we as individual Christians and the Church as a whole be saying and doing regarding all the varied aspects of human sexuality?

First and foremost, we need to proclaim, endorse and support that which God has established and sanctioned for our benefit. He has ordained a life-long, one man/one woman, marriage relationship (Mark 10:6-9) that is the foundation upon which a family is built and in turn becomes the basis for community and society. People, young and old, need to be encouraged to discipline themselves according to God's commands before marriage; to prepare for and enter marriage with the clear understanding of the length and depth of commitment required (Eph 5:28-32); and to live their lives in such a way as to bring honor to God, themselves and their spouse (Heb 13:4, Mat 5:31-32).

With regard to the sinful use of sexuality, the Church must state clearly and resolutely that it is wrong. We dare not take the responsibility upon ourselves to modify or ignore what God has said, regardless of how loudly advocated or commonplace a sinful practice has become! Failure to stand against these sins and proclaim the grace of God and His forgiveness leaves people drowning in their sin - separated from Jesus.[71]

Appendix XI: "Homosexuality" from Merton Strommen

All people are loved by God. All struggle with moral failure and fall short of God's standards; and therefore need the forgiveness that God provides through Christ alone. Homosexuality is but one of these struggles. While recognizing the need to reach out in love to those struggling with same sex attraction, CMDA opposes the practice of homosexual acts on biblical, medical, and social grounds.

BIBLICAL

- The Scriptures prescribe and promise God's blessing on life-long heterosexual union in marriage, and chastity in all other circumstances. They are uniform throughout in forbidding the practice of homosexuality.
- Same-sex attraction cannot be consummated within God's design for human sexuality. It is possible by God's grace for those with same sex attraction to live a chaste life. Choosing to indulge in homosexual acts in thought or deed is sinful. The Scriptures, however, affirm the value of non-erotic same-sex friendships.
- Any lifestyle obsessed with and/or dominated by personal sexual fulfillment, whether heterosexual or homosexual, is contrary to God's law.
- Homosexual acts deny the God-designed complementary nature of the sexes and do not have the potential to be procreative.

MEDICAL

- The causes of same-sex attraction appear to be multi-factorial and may include developmental, psychosocial, environmental and biological factors. There is no credible evidence at this time that same-sex attraction is genetically determined.
- Acting on homosexual attraction is voluntary. Claims of genetic or environmental determinism do not relieve individuals of moral responsibility for their sexual behavior.
- Homosexual behavior can be changed. There is valid evidence that many individuals who desired to abstain from homosexual acts have been able to do so.
- Some homosexual acts are physically harmful because they disregard normal human anatomy and function. These acts are associated with increased risks of tissue injury, organ malfunction, and infectious diseases. These and other factors result in a significantly shortened life expectancy.
- Among those involved in homosexual acts, there is an increased incidence of drug and/or alcohol dependence, compulsive sexual behavior, anxiety, depression, and suicide.

SOCIAL

- Homosexual relationships are typically brief in duration. Homosexual behavior is destructive to the structures necessary for healthy marriages, families and society. Men who commit homosexual acts have a high incidence of promiscuity, child molestation, and sexually transmitted infections. Homosexual behaviors burden society with increased medical costs, increased disability, and loss of productivity.
- Homosexual behavior can be self-propagating. Some homosexual groups and individuals engage in active recruitment. A child who is sexually molested has an increased likelihood of later engaging in homosexual acts. There is also an increased incidence of homosexual activity among children raised by same sex couples. Adoption into such environments puts children at risk.
- Legalizing or blessing same sex marriage or civil unions is harmful to the stability of society, the raising of children and the institution of marriage. If the only criterion for marriage were mutual consent or commitment, there are no grounds to prohibit polygamy, polyandry or incestuous unions.

CONCLUSION

- The Christian community must respond to the complex issues surrounding homosexuality with grace, civility, and love.
- Christian doctors in particular must care for their patients involved in homosexual behavior in a non-discriminating and compassionate manner, consistent with biblical principles.
- Anyone struggling with homosexual temptation should evoke neither scorn nor enmity, but evoke our concern, compassion, help, and understanding.
- The Christian community must condemn hatred and violence directed against those involved in the homosexual behavior.
- The Christian community must help society understand that homosexuality has grave spiritual, emotional, physical and cultural consequences. Christians should oppose legislative attempts to grant special rights based on sexual behavior or to equate homosexual relationships with heterosexual marriages.
- The Christian community and especially the family must resist stereotyping and rejecting individuals who do not fit the popular norms of masculinity and femininity. Also, it is important for parents to guide their children in appropriate gender identity development. For children who are experiencing gender identity confusion, we must provide appropriate role models, and therapy if needed.
- The Christian community must encourage and strongly support all those who wish to abandon homosexual behavior.

- The Christian community should oppose the legalization of same sex marriage and/or blessing and adoption into homosexual environments.
- God provides the remedy for all moral failure through faith in Jesus Christ and the life changing power of the Holy Spirit.[72]

Appendix XII--ELCA "Partners" in Corporate Responsibility[73]

Full Communion Partners
Relationships of full communion have been adopted with other church bodies
Affiliated Lutheran Partners
ELCA Board of Pensions, ELCA Foundation, Lutheran Immigration and
Refugee Service, Lutheran Services in America, Lutheran World Federation,
Lutheran World Relief

Protestant Socially Responsible Investing Partners
American Baptist Church
Church of the Brethren
Brethren Benefit Trust
The Episcopal Church
The Episcopal Church – Social Responsibility Investment Committee
The Mennonite Church
Mennonite Mutual Aid
Presbyterian Church (U.S.A.)
PC(U.S.A.) Mission Responsibility Through Investment
Unitarian Universalist Association
Unitarian Universalist Service Committee
United Church of Christ
The Pension Boards – United Church of Christ
The United Methodist Church
General Board of Global Ministries of The United Methodist Church
General Board of Pension and Health Benefits of the United Methodist Church
United Methodist Foundation

Ecumenical and Interfaith Partners
Christian Churches Together in U.S.A. ; Churches Uniting in Christ; Interfaith
Center on Corporate Responsibility; National Council of Churches in Christ
USA; World Council of Churches
Program Partners
CANICCOR; Center for Reflection Education and Advocacy
Equal Exchange; Rugmark Foundation
Investing Partners
Boston Common Asset Management, LLC; Domini Social Investments;
Oikocredit; Trillium Asset Management

Appendix XIII

Collin Raye » That's My Story Lyrics[74]

This song is sung by a husband who tells of being confronted by his wife as he comes in the door after being "out all night."

Time and again he tries various "stories" on her, thinking that one of them will provide the excuse he needs. Every time he tells one of those "stories," the song goes to the refrain:

That's my story. Oh, that's my story.
Well, I ain't got a witness, and I can't prove it,
but that's my story and I'm stickin' to it."

The wife refutes his stories one after another. Yet the husband just can't help but offer up lie after lie: "He's got a story and he's stickin' to it."

Appendix XIV--Justified by grace through faith

As Lutherans, we believe that we are justified by grace through faith. The Lutheran Confessions guide us in our understanding of justification by identifying three intersecting affirmations: *solus Christus, sola gratia,* and *sola fide* (Christ alone, grace alone, and by faith alone). *(see note below)* Deeply grounded in Scripture, understood as the living Word of God, these together proclaim
Jesus Christ as central to the Gospel:

• *Solus Christus* (Christ alone) insists that the purpose of Scripture is to reveal Jesus Christ as the Savior of the world. Scripture is to be interpreted through the lens of Christ's death and resurrection for the salvation of all.

• *Sola gratia* (grace alone) affirms that we are saved by grace alone. As with *solus Christus, sola gratia* means that there is nothing a person can do through his or her action that will create a right relationship with God. Only God's grace can do that.

• *Sola fide* (by faith alone) affirms that, through the hearing of God's Word, the Holy Spirit ignites faith (trust) in God within us

These three emphases also tell us that sin does not have to do simply with the keeping or breaking of rules or laws. Rather, we sin when we turn away from God and look to ourselves. Sin turns us toward obsessive self-concern, with disastrous consequences for ourselves and others.

--From 2009 ELCA Social Statement
"Human Sexuality: Gift and Trust"[75]

NOTE:*Each "sola" points to the same saving event. That is, they together proclaim Jesus Christ as central to the Gospel, each perceived from a different dimension. Other dimensions of God's saving work, other "solas," also have been associated with Lutheranism. Especially in the nineteenth century, Lutherans began to emphasize sola Scriptura, although the Confessions rarely used that phrase. Luther more often spoke of the Word of God alone (soli Verbo), by which he meant fundamentally the oral proclamation of the Gospel. For a key source suggesting the solas listed here, see Apology of the Augsburg Confession, IV. 120 in: The Book of Concord: The Confessions of the Evangelical Lutheran Church, eds. Robert Kolb and Timothy J. Wengert (Minneapolis: Fortress Press, 2000), hereafter referred to as "BC 2000."*

Appendix XV--MENDING WALL[76]
--Robert Frost

Something there is that doesn't love a wall,
That sends the frozen-ground-swell under it,
And spills the upper boulders in the sun,
And makes gaps even two can pass abreast.
The work of hunters is another thing:
I have come after them and made repair
Where they have left not one stone on a stone,
But they would have the rabbit out of hiding,
To please the yelping dogs. The gaps I mean,
No one has seen them made or heard them made,
But at spring mending-time we find them there.
I let my neighbor know beyond the hill;
And on a day we meet to walk the line
And set the wall between us once again.
We keep the wall between us as we go.
To each the boulders that have fallen to each.
And some are loaves and some so nearly balls
We have to use a spell to make them balance:
'Stay where you are until our backs are turned!'
We wear our fingers rough with handling them.
Oh, just another kind of out-door game,
One on a side. It comes to little more:
There where it is we do not need the wall:
He is all pine and I am apple orchard.
My apple trees will never get across
And eat the cones under his pines, I tell him.
He only says, 'Good fences make good neighbors'.
Spring is the mischief in me, and I wonder
If I could put a notion in his head:
'Why do they make good neighbors? Isn't it
Where there are cows?
But here there are no cows.
Before I built a wall I'd ask to know
What I was walling in or walling out,
And to whom I was like to give offence.
Something there is that doesn't love a wall,
That wants it down.' I could say 'Elves' to him,
But it's not elves exactly, and I'd rather
He said it for himself. I see him there
Bringing a stone grasped firmly by the top
In each hand, like an old-stone savage armed.
He moves in darkness as it seems to me~

Not of woods only and the shade of trees.
He will not go behind his father's saying,
And he likes having thought of it so well
He says again, "Good fences make good neighbors."

Appendix XVI Word Alone & Lutheran CORE

Word Alone's primary concern is that the ELCA is losing its Christ-centered focus. ELCA churches and members are turning to authorities other than the authority of God's Word, revealed in his risen Son, Jesus Christ, and in his inspired Word in the Holy Scriptures. The other authorities – human experience, wisdom and tradition – are used to turn aside the authority of God's Word. The weaknesses within the ELCA – ecumenical agreements that compromise on significant biblical and confessional truths, the teaching and preaching of universalism, a decline in the proper mission of the church (global missions and new mission starts) and the push for approval of sexual relationships outside of marriage to name just a few – are symptoms of the deeper problem within the ELCA, the crisis over the authority of God's Word.

WordAlone Network & Lutheran CORE
2299 Palmer Drive
Suite #220
New Brighton, MN 55112
651.633.6004
fax 651.633.4260
toll-free 888.551.7254
wordalone@popp.net

Lutheran CORE is a coalition of pastors, lay people, congregations and reforming groups. We seek to preserve within the Lutheran churches in North America the authority of the Word of God according to the Lutheran confessions. Our intention is to work with congregations, individuals, and other reform-minded groups for the renewal of churches, by:
1. Encouraging individual reform-minded congregations, laypersons, and pastors.
2. Supporting and offering coordination for the various Lutheran renewal groups in North America.
3. Addressing significant theological issues.

Appendix XVII--Augsburg Lutheran Churches and LCMC

Augsburg Lutheran Churches

Are you looking for a way to connect in a Christ centered, Gospel driven, Bible teaching community? Augsburg Lutheran Churches is a fellowship of churches, chapters, and confessors united by a common confession of faith in Jesus Christ.

Our Mission

To bear witness to the good news that sinners are put right with God by faith alone in Christ alone. We resist any corruption of this Gospel, and exist to serve and support fellow confessors who seek to do likewise. Looking only to the cross of Christ, we proclaim God's Word as Law and Gospel for the redemption of his people today. May God help us to the glory of His holy name. Amen.

http://www.augsburgchurches.org/

Lutheran Congregations in Mission for Christ

Lutheran Congregations in Mission for Christ is an association of congregations and individuals who are: 1)free in Christ; 2) accountable to one another; 3) rooted in the Scriptures and the Lutheran Confessions; 4) working together to fulfill Christ's Great Commission to go and make disciples of all nations. LCMC is an association of congregations. We have a great respect for the reality that the church is where the people of God gather together around Word and Sacrament. The local congregation is where the church becomes a concrete reality for God's people.

At the same time we are joyously aware that each congregation is a part of the greater body of Christ. The actions of each congregation within our association reflect on our association as a whole. And the actions of our association reflect on the whole body of Christ. For this reason we have committed ourselves to a common set of ministry standards.

Congregations have significant latitude in ordering and shaping ministry in their local setting, and we intentionally have made joining and leaving the association simple. We have also agreed to a disciplinary process for addressing congregations whose actions violate our agreed-upon statements of faith and practice.

http://www.lcmc.net/

Appendix XVIII — Constitution and By-law protections

Possible Amendments to Congregation's Constitution
These amendments address significant issues resulting from the actions of the 2009 ELCA Churchwide Assembly. They could be included in a congregation's constitution or bylaws. The numbers indicate where the amendment would go in a constitution similar to the ELCA Model Constitution for Congregations.
Amendment C2.08
Accepts The Common Confession as a summary of Lutheran teaching including the following statements that directly address significant issues resulting from the ELCA actions:
1. Defines marriage as between a man and a woman and as created by God and clearly states that "sexual activity belongs exclusively within the biblical boundaries of a faithful marriage between one man and one woman."
2. States that "The Bible is the final authority for us in all matters of our faith and life."
Amendment C6.07
Establishes a relationship between congregation and Lutheran CORE.
Amendment C9.15
Uses language from the ELCA document, "Vision and expectations," prior to the actions of the 2009 Churchwide Assembly to state the expectation that pastors of this congregation must maintain traditional Christian teaching on marriage sexuality in their ministry actions and in their personal behavior.
Amendment C9.16
Uses language from the 1993 ELCA Conference of Bishops Statement — that was affirmed by the 2005 ELCA Churchwide Assembly — to state that the congregation will not offer same-sex marriage or blessing services.
Amendments to Chapter 12
The wording of many portions of the ELCA Model Constitution for Congregations is required and may not be edited as a long as congregation is in the ELCA. The exact wording of sections in Chapter 12 are not required by the ELCA. Additions are underlined and deletions are indicated by strikeouts. These significant changes could be made to Chapter 12:
C12.04 would indicate that the actions of the Congregation Council are done in accordance with the Confession of Faith of the congregation rather than the faith and practice of the ELCA.
C12.04h changes reference to the synod and churchwide organization to a reference to "other Lutherans both locally and globally" and removes the requirement that working with other congregations is "subject to established policies of the synod and ELCA."
C12.04i removes a requirement that the Congregation Council "recommend and encourage the use of program resources produced or approved by the ELCA." Given the changes in ELCA teaching and practice, congregations will want flexibility in choosing what resources to use.
C2.08. This congregation accepts The Common Confession as a summary of teachings in the Lutheran Confessions:
C6.07. This congregation shall be a member of the Lutheran Coalition for Renewal (Lutheran CORE).
C9.15. Ordained ministers, whether married or single, are expected to uphold an understanding of marriage in their public ministry as well as in private life that is biblically informed and
consistent with the teachings of this congregation. The expectations of this congregation regarding the sexual conduct of its ordained ministers are grounded in the understanding that

human sexuality is a gift from God and that ordained ministers are to live in such a way as to honor this gift. Ordained ministers are expected to reject sexual promiscuity, the manipulation
of others for purposes of sexual gratification, and all attempts of sexual seduction and sexual harassment, including taking physical or emotional advantage of others. Single ordained
ministers are expected to live a chaste life. Married ordained ministers are expected to live in fidelity to their spouses, giving expression to sexual intimacy within a marriage relationship that
is mutual, chaste, and faithful. Ordained ministers who are homosexual in their self-understanding are expected to abstain from homosexual sexual relationships.
C9.16. Marriage is a lifelong covenant of faithfulness between a man and a woman. There is basis neither in Scripture nor tradition for the establishment of an official ceremony by the Church for the blessing of a homosexual relationship. We, therefore, do not approve such a ceremony as an official action of this congregation's ministry either on its property or by its pastors.

Section 5 – SUBSCRIBERS

Instructions:
If you have been moved to confession, then join me and other confessiors "in statu confessionis" – STAND AND CONFESS!

You can do so by signing your name to this confession and to other confessors' confession. Fill up these pages with confessing names!

You can go to:
www.standandconfess.blogspot.com
Read the post there, find the "comments" link at the bottom of the post, click on it, and leave your name and any other contact information or pertinent comments you care to make.

You can request more copies of "Stand and Confess"
Or request that your name be added to the "confessors" list
Or request additional information by emailing:
camelhairshirt@yahoo.com

or by calling:
1-701-566-8128

You can visit St. Martin's School of Theological Discernment
http://stmartiesplace.blogspot.com/

END NOTES

[1] *"We believe, teach, and confess that in a time of persecution, when an unequivocal confession of the faith is demanded of us, we dare not yield to the opponents in such indifferent matters. As the Apostle wrote, 'Stand firm in the freedom for which Christ has set us free, and do not submit again to a yoke of slavery' [Gal. 5:1]. And: 'Do not put on the yoke of others; what partnership is there between light and darkness?' [2 Cor. 6:14]. 'So that the truth of the Gospel might always remain with you, we did not submit to them even for a moment' [Gal. 2:5]. For in such a situation it is no longer indifferent matters that are at stake. The truth of the gospel and Christian freedom are at stake. The confirmation of open idolatry, as well as the protection of the weak in faith from offense, is at stake. In such matters we can make no concessions but must offer an unequivocal confession and suffer whatever God sends and permits the enemies of His Word to inflict on us"* [Formula of Concord-Epitome, Article X,6].
http://reformationtoday.tripod.com/chemnitz/id11.html
(accessed 2009-11-30

[2] Nestingen, James Arne, "Joining the Unchurched"
http://wordalone.org/docs/nestingen-joining-unchurched.shtml
(accessed 2009-12-05)

[3] Heinlein, Robert A., Take Back Your Government
http://www.amazon.com/gp/product/0671721577?ie=UTF8&tag=wwwviolentkicom
&link_code=as3&camp=211189&creative=373489&creativeASIN=0671721577wwwvi
olentkicom
(accessed 2009-12-01)

[4] Luther, Martin, Explanation to the 3rd Article of the Apostles' Creed, the Small Catechism
http://www.iclnet.org/pub/resources/text/wittenberg/luther/little.book/book-2.txt
(accessed 2009-12-01)

[5] Hillerbrand, Hans, "*Status Confessionis*—Reflections on an Evasive Concept"—a paper delivered at 2009 Word Alone Theological Conference

[6] P. 10 ELCA Social Statement "Human Sexuality: Gift and Trust"

[7] Also they teach that one holy Church is to continue forever. The Church is the congregation of saints, in which the Gospel is rightly taught and the Sacraments are rightly administered.
And to the true unity of the Church it is enough to agree concerning the doctrine of the Gospel and the administration of the Sacraments. Nor is it necessary that human traditions, that is, rites or ceremonies, instituted by men, should be everywhere alike. As Paul says: One faith, one Baptism, one God and Father of all, etc. Eph. 4, 5. 6.
http://www.iclnet.org/pub/resources/text/wittenberg/concord/web/augs-007.html
(accessed 2009-11-30)

[8] Nestingen, James Arne, "Joining the Unchurched"
http://www.wordalone.org/docs/nestingen-joining-unchurched.shtml
(accessed 2009-11-30)

[9] Nestingen, James Arne "The Necessity of Resistance"
http://www.wordalone.org/pdf/Nestingen-Necessity-of-Resistance-in-2009.pdf
(accessed2009-11-30)

[10] Wikipedia http://en.wikipedia.org/wiki/Orthodox

(accessed 2009-12-01)

[11] Wikipedia http://en.wikipedia.org/wiki/Heterodoxy
(accessed 2009-12-01)

[12] Wikipedia http://en.wikipedia.org/wiki/Heresy
(accessed 2009-12-01)

[13] Wikipedia http://en.wikipedia.org/wiki/Schism_(religion)
(accessed 2009-12-01)

[14] Wikipedia http://en.wikipedia.org/wiki/Apostasy
(accessed 2009-12-01

[15] Heiser, The Rev. James D., pastor: "Pastoral Responsibility and the Office of the Keys in the Book of Concord"
http://www.reformationtoday.net/sitebuildercontent/sitebuilderfiles/pastoralrespon sibility.pdf
(accessed 2009-11-30)

[16] Heinlein, Robert A., Take Back Your Government
http://www.amazon.com/gp/product/0671721577?ie=UTF8&tag=wwwviolentkicom &link_code=as3&camp=211189&creative=373489&creativeASIN=0671721577wwwvi olentkicom
(accessed 2009-12-01)

[17] Luther, Martin, Explanation to the 3rd Article of the Apostles' Creed, the Small Catechism
http://www.iclnet.org/pub/resources/text/wittenberg/luther/little.book/book-2.txt
(accessed 2009-12-01)

[18] "Social statements are social policy documents, adopted by an ELCA Churchwide Assembly, addressing significant social issues. They provide an analysis and interpretation of an issue, set forth basic theological and ethical perspectives related to it, and offer guidance for the Evangelical Lutheran Church in America, its individual members, and its affiliated agencies and institutions. They are the product of extensive and inclusive deliberation within this church. Since 1991, the ELCA has adopted ten social statements."
http://www.elca.org/What-We-Believe/Social-Issues/Social-Statements.aspx
(accessed 11-23-2009)

[19] http://www.elca.org/What-We-Believe/Social-Issues/Social-Statements/JTF-Human-Sexuality.aspx (accessed 11-23-2009) read down the page until you come to "social statement text," click there for a PDF of the document

[20] P. 10, ELCA Social Statement: "Human Sexuality: Gift and Trust"

[21] http://www.elca.org/Growing-In-Faith/Vocation/Rostered-Leadership/Ministry-Policies.aspx (accessed 11-23-2009) read down the page until you find "Process for Fulfilling..." then click on the link word "directed" for the text of the recommendations.

[22] "This documents uses the terms "marriage "and "married" to refer to marriage between one man and woman. "Human Sexuality: Gift and Trust" has the same usage but acknowledges (p. ....) that some in this church understand the term as being

appropriate also for the relationship of a same-gender couple." Draft Amendments to Vision and Expectations (10/10/09) http://www.elca.org/Growing-In-Faith/Vocation/Rostered-Leadership/Ministry-Policies.aspx (accessed 11-23-2009)
[23]Human Sexuality: Gift and Trust," p.11
http://www.elca.org/~/media/Files/Who%20We%20Are/Office%20of%20the%20Secretary/Assembly/CWA%202009%20Revised%20Social%20Statement%20HSGT%20FINAL%20090309.pdf
(accessed 2009-12-03)
[24] Nestingen, James Arne "The Necessity of Resistance"
http://wordalone.org/pdf/Nestingen-Necessity-of-Resistance-in-2009.pdf (accessed 2009-12-06)
[25] Wallis, Louis, Sociological Study of the Bible, p. 164ff
http://www.amazon.com/Sociological-Study-Bible-Louis-Wallis/dp/1406708658
(accessed 2009-12-01)
[26] Rabin, Elliot, Understanding the Hebrew Bible: a reader's guide, p155ff
http://www.amazon.com/Understanding-Hebrew-Bible-Readers-Guide/dp/0881258717 (accessed 2009-12-01)
[27] http://en.wikipedia.org/wiki/Lex_orandi,_lex_credendi (accessed 2009-12-05)
[28] Madson, Meg H. "What's at Stake?"
http://wordalone.org/docs/wa-whats-at-stake.shtml (accessed 2009-12-05)
[29] http://www.elca.org/Our-Faith-In-Action/Justice/Advocacy/Advocacy-Ministries/ELCA-Washington-Office.aspx
(accessed 2009-12-03)
[30] http://www.elca.org/Our-Faith-In-Action/Justice/Advocacy/Corporate-Social-Responsibility/ABOUT-CSR-MAIN-PAGE.aspx
(accessed 2009-12-03)
[31] (Constitution of the World Council of Churches, Article III)
http://www.oikoumene.org/documentation/themes/unite-des-chretiens.html
(accessed 2009-12-02)
[32] Preface to BEM
http://www.oikoumene.org/resources/documents/wcc-commissions/faith-and-order-commission/i-unity-the-church-and-its-mission/baptism-eucharist-and-ministry-faith-and-order-paper-no-111-the-lima-text.html
(accessed 2009-12-02)
[33] http://www.oikoumene.org/documentation/themes/unite-des-chretiens.html#c26974
(accessed 2009-12-02)
[34] http://www.elca.org/Who-We-Are/Our-Three-Expressions/Churchwide-Organization/Office-of-the-Secretary/ELCA-Governance/Constitutions-of-the-Evangelical-Lutheran-Church-in-America.aspx
(accessed 2009-12-02)
[35] "The Vision of the Evangelical Lutheran Church in America" Part 2, p.3, item 4

http://www.elca.org/Who-We-Are/Our-Three-Expressions/Churchwide-Organization/Ecumenical-and-Inter-Religious-Relations/Who-we-are.aspx
(accessed 2009-12-02)

[36] The Vision of the Evangelical Lutheran Church in America

[37] http://www.elca.org/Who-We-Are/Our-Three-Expressions/Churchwide-Organization/Ecumenical-and-Inter-Religious-Relations/Full-Communion/Presbyterian-Church-USA/A-Formula-of-Agreement.aspx
(accessed 2009-12-02

[38] Miller, Pastor Gerald, "A confessional protest regarding—the ELCA's adoption of "Called to Common Mission"
http://wordalone.org/docs/wa-confessional-protest.shtml (accessed 2009-12-05)

[39] Menacher, Mark, "CCM, the Grand Deception"
http://www.ccmverax.org/GrandDeception.htm (accessed 2009-12-05)

[40] http://www.elca.org/Who-We-Are/Our-Three-Expressions/Churchwide-Organization/Ecumenical-and-Inter-Religious-Relations/Bilateral-Conversations/Lutheran-Roman-Catholic/Doctrine-of-Justification-LWF-and-Catholic-Church/The-Joint-Declaration.aspx
(accessed 2009-12-03)

[41] The Joint Declaration on the Doctrine of Justification, paragraph 5

[42] 1 The Smalcald Articles, II,1; Book of Concord, 292.

[43] Turretin, Francis, 1682 http://turretinfan.blogspot.com/2009/03/lutherjustification-is-stand-or-fall.html (accessed 2009-12-03)

[44] Preus, Rolf, "JDDJ Ten Years Later—The Historic Divide Endures"
http://www.logia.org/index.php?option=com_content&view=article&id=97&catid=39:web-forum&Itemid=18
(accessed 2009-12-03)

[45] Stanly, Alessandra, "Urging Millennial Penitence, Pope is Offering Indulgences" The New York Times, December 3, 1998
http://www.nytimes.com/1998/11/28/world/urging-millennial-penitence-pope-is-offering-indulgences.html
(accessed 2009-12-03)

[46] http://www.elca.org/

[47] Swenson, Timothy J. King, Stephen, "A Reader's Guide to Luther's Catechisms"
SOLA Publishing
http://www.solapublishing.org/

[48] Culver, Jim, "The Good, the Bad, and the Ugly"
http://wordalone.org/docs/wa-king-culver.shtml
(accessed 2009-12-03)

[49] Swenson, Timothy J, "The Impossibility and Inevitability of Good Works"
http://noontology.blogspot.com/ (accessed 2009-12-03)

[50] Luther, Martin, Explanation to Baptism in the Small Catechism
http://www.iclnet.org/pub/resources/text/wittenberg/luther/little.book/book-4.txt
(accessed 2009-12-01)

[51] Nestingen, James Arne, "Reflections on the Past in Hopes of an Alternate Future" http://www.wordalone.org/t/nestingen-2002.doc (accessed 2009-12-03)

[52] Leviticus 18:22; Leviticus 20:13; Romans 1:26-27; 1 Corinthians 6:9; 1 Timothy 1:10—and others

[53] Lev. 21:9; 19:29; Deut. 22:20, 21, 23-29; 23:18; Ex. 22:16—and others

[54] Ex. 20:14 Deut. 5:18; Matt. 5:27; 19:18; Luke 18:20; Rom. 13:9—and others

[55] Lev. 18:6-18; Lev. 20:11, 12, 17, 19-21; Deut. 22:30; Deut. 27:20, 22, 23; Ezek. 22:11; 1 Cor. 5:1—and others

[56] Lev.18:6-18—the paucity of passages condemning this behavior does not reflect scripture's silence on the matter but that the behavior was so universally condemned it's practice was virtually unthinkable

[57] Ex. 22:19; Lev. 18:23; Lev. 20:16; Deut. 27:2

[58] Lev. 19:29; Deut. 23:17; 31:16; Judg. 2:17; 2 Kin. 9:22.

[59] Gen 38:8-10

[60] Mat. 5:32; Mar. 10:12; Luk. 16:18; Lev. 21:7—and others

[61] Gen. 2:23, 24 1 Cor. 6:16. Ex. 22:16, 17; Lev. 18:6-8 [Deut. 22:30.] Lev. 18:9-18; Lev. 20:14, 17, 19-21; Lev. 21:1, 7, 13-15; Num. 36:8; Deut. 21:10-14; Deut. 24:1-5; Prov. 18:22; Prov. 21:9, 19; Jer. 29:6; Hos. 2:19, 20; Mal. 2:13-16; Matt. 5:31, 32; Mark 6:17, 18; Mark 10:2-12 Matt. 19:2-9. Luke 16:18; Rom. 7:1-3; 1 Cor. 7:1-40; 1 Cor. 9:5; 1 Cor. 11:11, 12; 1 Tim. 3:2, 12; 1 Tim. 4:1, 3; 1 Tim. 5:14; Heb. 13:4

[62] Scripture often labels the frequent and wanton engagement in this variety of forbidden sexual expressions under such terms as "promiscuity," "licentiousness," "lasciviousness," and "sexual immorality"

[63] Paulson, Steven D., "How to Preach Galatians—law and gospel not acceptance and inclusion" http://wordalone.org/docs/wa-paulson-2007.shtml (accessed 2009-12-05)

[64] The Constitution of the ELCA http://www.elca.org/Who-We-Are/Our-Three-Expressions/Churchwide-Organization/Office-of-the-Secretary/ELCA-Governance/Constitutions-of-the-Evangelical-Lutheran-Church-in-America.aspx (accessed 2009-11-30)

[65] Ministry Rites in the ELCA http://www.elca.org/Growing-In-Faith/Worship/Resources/Ministry-Rites.aspx (accessed 2009-12-01)

[66] "The Necessity of Resistance" http://www.wordalone.org/docs/wa-resistance.shtml (accessed 2009-12-01)

[67] The Book of Concord: The Confessions of the Evangelical Lutheran Church; translated and edited by Theodore G. Tappert, Fortress Press, 1959

[68] Swenson, Timothy J., "The End of Being" 2006-02-27 http://noontology.blogspot.com/ (accessed 2009-12-02)

[69] http://www2.elca.org/lutheranpartners/archives/histepi.html (accessed 2009-12-02)

[70] Nestingen, James Arne, "Authority and Resistance in the ELCA" http://www.wordalone.org/docs/wa-authority-resistance-elca.shtml (Accessed 2009-12-03)

[71] Strommen, Merton, "A Biblical Approach to Homosexuality" http://www.wordalone.org/docs/wa-biblical-approach.shtml (accessed 2009-12-07)

[72] Strommen, Merton, "Homosexuality" http://www.wordalone.org/docs/wa-homosexuality.shtml (Accessed 2009-12-03)

[73] http://www.elca.org/Our-Faith-In-Action/Justice/Advocacy/Corporate-Social-Responsibility/PARTNERS-MAIN-PAGE.aspx (accessed 2009-12-03)

[74] http://www.lyricsdomain.com/3/collin_raye/thats_my_story.html (accessed 2009-12-03)

[75] http://www.elca.org/~/media/Files/Who%20We%20Are/Office%20of%20the%20Secretary/Assembly/CWA%202009%20Revised%20Social%20Statement%20HSGT%20FINAL%20090309.pdf (accessed 2009-12-03)

[76] http://www.poets.org/viewmedia.php/prmMID/15719 (accessed 2009-12-07)